500 SEC

Essential Strategies To Bulldoze Through Google's Rankings, Increase Traffic and Go Viral

Silvia O'Dwyer

Copyright © 2015 by Silvia O'Dwyer
All Rights Reserved

No part of this book may be reproduced in any form by any means without prior permission from the author. This includes reprints, excerpts or any future means of reproducing text.

Several logos have been included in this book. The author of this book identifies the owner of the logos, and that the logo is not authorized by, sponsored by or associated with the trademark owner.

DISCLAIMER

The author of this book and accompanying resources have made best efforts in creating this book. The author makes no representation or warranties with respect to the accuracy, completeness or of the contents of this book. The information within this book is for educational purposes only. Therefore, if you apply these ideas you take full responsibility for your actions. The author is in no way held liable to any party for any direct, indirect, special or incidental damages arising directly or indirectly from any use of this material.

Printed by CreateSpace Independent Publishing Platform
Cover designed by Armend Meha (www.armend.org)

ISBN-13: 978-1511612722
ISBN-10: 151161272X

Version 1.1 (Polaris)

Table of Contents

Chapter 1: Keyword Research *6*

Chapter 2: Competition Analysis *23*

Chapter 3: On-Page SEO *31*

Chapter 4: Linkbuilding *41*

Chapter 5: Prospering In A Post Panda and Penguin World *84*

Chapter 6: Technical SEO *93*

Chapter 7: Local SEO *108*

Chapter 8: Predictions For 2020 *114*

Chapter 9: Content Marketing *120*

Chapter 10: Visual Content Marketing *146*

Chapter 11: Incredible Tips From The SEO Experts *159*

Chapter 12: Common SEO Myths *178*

Chapter 13: SEO Philosophy *200*

A Quick Intro to 500 SEO Tips

Do you want to start getting traffic to your site and fast? Do you need lots of invaluable, juicy tips to get your website ranking higher? Want to get your website known on the web alongside brands such as Mashable and Buzzfeed?

"500 SEO Tips" is an answer to every webmaster's call.

It's time to go viral, get known and rank higher.

It's time to start getting insanely actionable advice that you can use right now, to get your website on the road to extremely successful.

"500 SEO Tips" contains 500 bite-sized yet extremely actionable SEO strategies, tips, tricks, tools and hacks that you can use right now.

A lot of the advice on the web is difficult to read and completely outdated. This book offers you the complete course to SEO. Retaining all that experience but completely up to date for 2015.

Most of the tips found in this book can't be found on the web. Simple as that.

I've also asked some of the most notable experts in SEO, and a few industry leaders to give their thoughts on the best SEO tips they've ever come across.

A Sampler of What You'll Learn

Here are a few of the things that you'll get access to once you buy the book:
- How To Get Wikipedia Backlinks
- How To Get Your Website Featured By Journalists and Influencers
- The Google Keyword Planner "Hack" That'll Get You Thousands of Profitable Keywords
- How To Rank First For An Incredibly Competitive Keyword

- Get 50+ backlinks to one piece of content using "The HARO Hack"
- 40 SEO Strategies That Are A Complete Waste of Time
- The One Technical Issue That's Pulling Your Website Back In The Rankings
- The Definitive Guide To Getting Published On The Huffington Post and Forbes
- How To Create Infographics That Go Viral, and Will Be Reposted On Major Websites
- Predictions for SEO in 2020

Get exclusive access to these tips plus hundreds more!
Don't waste any more time, buy this book today and join thousands who are propelling their websites to the top of Google right now!

Why You Should Read This Book

Kudos to you for choosing to take a look at this book! You're already on the path to getting more traffic from Google and building a highly successful website. During the course of writing this book, I received an email from a content creator I recently contacted. Here's what she said:

*"You know what? Don't bother writing this book, scrap it. Instead of writing the book, become a
content marketer and charge webmasters hundreds for your content. That's the best option, in my opinion."*

I've done the complete opposite to what she recommended.

I've mentioned every last hack, trick and tip that has ever existed in the SEO world.

And, no I'm not going to charge you hundreds for them. They're in your hand, ready to be tapped into.
So go out there. Follow these tips. Create something amazing, and get it the exposure it deserves.

No more fluff. No more babble. From now on, it's just extremely useful SEO tips.

CHAPTER 1

Keyword Research

A keyword is the word or more often, words that people type into Google's search bar. For example, "how to build a circuit". If you write an article about "How to Build a Circuit", your article will rank in the results of selected pages that Google wishes to show.

Certain keywords tend to do better than others. The most successful webmasters and bloggers know what kinds of topics to target. Some are profitable and easy to rank, whilst others can be easy to rank but not profitable. It is this knowledge which makes them so successful because once you rank high for a money-making keyword, your website will get more exposure than you can think of.

This chapter is all about helping you pick profitable keywords which you can use to rank higher. You will learn how to generate keywords, test how profitable they are and select the keywords which will make you the most money. You will then learn how to embed these keywords into your website, for best rankings.

How To Generate Hundreds of Keywords

1. Start A Keyword Mindmap
Your typical mind map consists of sub-headings stemming from the center. Let's use this simple idea to start our keyword generation. The keyword mind map consists of your main niche as the center and then sub-topics emitting from the center. Through this method, you will start with a basic seed keyword or phrase where you will add more sub-categories.

More categories will be generated to the sub-categories and by the end, you will have a full niche of keywords to write about whenever you like.

2. Create Your Keyword Mindmap

The first thing you need to do is to generate a single "seed keyword". This is basically your main niche, eg: smartphone security, British cooking or chemistry lessons.

Then, think of all the sub-topics associated with your niche.

Examples: British cooking could be divided into starters, main courses, snacks, drinks and desserts.
Chemistry lessons could be divided into the many topics of chemistry such as organic chemistry, particle science and so on.

3. Generate More Sub Niches With Wikipedia

As part of your hunt for topics to cover on your website or pages to create, you should also head over to Wikipedia. By searching for your niche, and looking at its page – you can find extra topics to write about or cover on your website. For example, if your website sells vitamins, you can create content on the types of vitamins, why they're so beneficial, impacts on the body and so forth. Those ideas came from the headings that Wikipedia covered on their page for vitamins.

4. Get A Keyword List With Ubersuggest

Your keyword mind map is the base for obtaining a keyword list in your niche. You need to get a sub-category on your mind map and start generating more keywords from that. Ubersuggest allows you to enter a "seed" keyword. It will then generate hundreds of new keywords based on that prime idea.
They use Google Suggest to obtain these keywords.

Google Suggest is the dropdown feature that pops up when you search something on Google. Keywords only get to this list if they are searched for at least ten times a month. Ubersuggest "scrapes" all of these keywords that Google have documented into their suggest feature.
You can add a single keyword and then get hundreds of suggestions. For example, if I type "Halloween" into Ubersuggest, I will get ten results with ["Halloween" + word beginning with a] such as "Halloween art", "Halloween accessories". Some of the keyword phrases suggested can be three, four or even five words.

To use this tool, head over to www.ubersuggest.com and input one of your sub-category words such as "organic chemistry" from the chemistry lessons example.

Add all of the generated keywords to your list by pressing the green plus sign beside each suggestion. Scroll up and click the "Get" button. Copy these and save them as a text file.

5. Generate More Keywords With Keywordtool.io

With this tool, you can add a single keyword and it will add extra words beginning with every letter of the alphabet. If I inputted "trees" into the tool, I would get results with "trees + word beginning with a". Numbers are also added onto the first word.

It generates on average, 700+ words and they are scraped from Google Suggest. The results are always different from Ubersuggest which means you can get a fresh batch of new keywords. I have found that some of the words were utter gibberish but here and there you will find some nice ideas.

Go to www.keywordtool.io and input your niche sub-category word (such as "cake baking" or "keyword research". Copy these to your clipboard (using the "Copy All button at the top) and head over to Word and paste them from your Clipboard into your Word document.

6. Generate "Buyer" Keywords With Soovle

Strange name, no doubt but this tool is exceptionally handy for scraping long tail keywords from multiple websites not just Google. Examples of these websites include Amazon, Wikipedia, Bing and Yahoo among many more. One single keyword into the tool will generate up to one hundred keywords from various channels.

This tool works exactly the same as Ubersuggest and keywordtool.io only that it scrapes these keywords from different channels not just Google. Whilst these keywords can be from eBay or Bing which we aren't focusing on, you can still use the keywords and check them out later on.

Check it out at www.soovle.com.

7. Steal Keywords From Your Competition

Every website has its own keyword strategies. You can steal these very easily. It isn't gaming the system, it's improving your own website! You can see what juicy keywords are sending traffic to their website.

If they have some "secret" keywords that are secretly bringing traffic to their website, you can use them for your own webpages and content.

Simply follow the GKP hack in tip #16. Instead of inputting the link of a blog post or Pinterest board, input their website link instead. Analyze the keywords and pick out any keywords that get more than 300 searches.

8. KWFinder Is Another Fantastic Way To Do Keyword Research

This tool is a complete dashboard for all your keyword research needs. All you have to do is search for a keyword, and then, the tool will give you about thirty keyword suggestions with all the metrics, a graph showing the interest in that keyword over time, the overall competition for that keyword, and who's ranking in the top ten for that keyword.

It isn't hugely extensive, you won't find as much keyword suggestions as you would with others but it does consolidate a lot of the work into one dashboard. The free version can be quite limited, but it still offers plenty of information. Try it now at www.kwfinder.com.

9. Mine Through Your Google Analytics Data

If your site has been running for more than a year, and you've gotten a good amount of search traffic over that time (in the tens of thousands), you can start mining through your Google Analytics data and see what keywords people actually used to get to your site. This can be one of the most valuable sources of keywords because those keywords are the ones which brought people, money and leads to your website.

Even if you have thousands of [not provided] keywords, you will still find a plethora of keywords which haven't been plagued by the [not provided] phenomenon. To start looking through your GA data now, simply log into your Google Analytics dashboard, select Acquisition>Campaigns>Organic Keywords.

10. Start A Keyword Ideas Folder

Create a new folder called Keyword Ideas and place it on your Desktop where you regularly see it. Every time you generate a new list of keywords from Ubersuggest or get the monthly searches for keywords from the Google Keyword Planner, you can save them in this folder.

You can even divide the folder into separate folders such as your keyword mind map sub-categories. You can add your lists of generated keywords into each folder and then the results from the Keyword Planner.

That way, you have all your keywords in one available resource!

11. Assemble All Your Keywords Into A File

Copy and paste all your generated keywords into a simple word document either using Word or Notepad or whatever. This makes it super quick to paste your keywords into the Google Keyword Planner later on.

How To Find Out Which Keywords Are The Most Profitable

12. Analyze Keywords With The Google Keyword Planner

Go to www.adwords.google.com and sign in with your Google Account or create an account if you don't have one. Once the page loads, you will see a page similar to the one below.

Head over to "Tools" on the top and select "Keyword Planner". Once the Keyword Planner has loaded up, click on the third option and paste in your list of generated keywords. The maximum number of keywords you can input is one thousand but you can submit an Excel file and analyze 3000 instead. Hit Submit.

For the keywords you inputted, you will see many terms which describe CPC, searches per month and more. Here is a quick guide to all those terms:

- **Searches** – This column tells you the number of searches a keyword phrase receives each month, globally. You would need a keyword to be receiving more than 1000 searches a month. This would equate to about 33 views a day for a new article which is a lot. Much debate goes into the number of searches that a keyword gets because some target 5,000 and others 10,000. It really depends on your level of SEO so for now, stick with the 500-2000 range.

- **Competition** – The Keyword Planner is originally designed for those who use AdWords, Google's advertising platform. By saying "competition", this refers to advertising competition. Advertisers placing ads on certain keywords pay more than others. When someone clicks on their ad, there is a set price for that ad depending on the keyword. This does not refer to the competition that websites have in search results.

If your website is a business and you want your visitors to convert well (becoming a customer), select keywords with a higher cost per click. This is because they are "business words", ie: keywords that bring customers who will convert rather than leave.

- **Suggested Bid** – This means "Cost per Click" and is the amount of money an advertiser would pay for one click of an advertisement to do with that keyword. Don't push yourself in writing articles with a high CPC, I generally wouldn't look at it as it has no impact on traffic.

13. The Stats You Should Aim For
You see all the stats about each keyword and wonder to yourself about which keywords are worth chasing. Basically you need to find keywords which are have the following monthly searches.
- **1000-4000 Monthly Searches:** The sweet zone is in this region simply because it will result in a large amount of traffic and competition won't be as high. 1000 monthly searches may not seem much when you break it down to a daily number but for a beginning website, 30 daily hits on one page is great.

If you wrote ten articles/created ten pages in the 1000 range where competition isn't tough, you will get about 300 people accessing your website every day! That is a lot for your business or website! Especially when you are starting out. Once you build up an authority, you can start aiming for higher monthly searches such as 2000 all the way up to 5000 (assuming that PR 1-3 websites are ranking).

14. Looking For "Product" Words?

The best way to find keywords that are going to lead to a higher conversion rate or higher rate of purchasing your products is to find keywords with a high CPC (cost per click) usually in the region from $3-12. However, the higher the CPC gets, the higher the competition becomes. So pick a keyword with a CPC that is typically in the $3 to $7 range. Anything above that range, and you'll find it impossible to rank for those keywords.

Since companies are bidding for these keywords (and are willing to spend their advertising budget on that keyword), it's clear that the people searching for this keyword have some cash to spend and need to do it pretty soon. You can see why those companies are desperate to get those searchers looking at their website.

15. Generate New Keywords Using GKP

As well as checking the potential of keywords, you can also generate new ones related to that niche. It is quick and easy to do this.

Go to www.adwords.google.com and sign in with your Google Account. Once the homepage loads, click on the Tools tab and then "Keyword Planner".

This will bring you to the Planner. Click on the First option and input some of your targeted keywords. Keep them fairly broad, eg: netbook accessories. You should get about 600+ keywords from this and you can download the list (if your computer can open CSV or Excel files). You can analyze them and pick a few golden nuggets of keywords.

16. Get Super Profitable Keywords No One Is Using Yet

This simple yet amazingly effective hack will give you highly profitable keywords that nobody has seen yet. This means that you can rank easily for these keywords and get huge traffic!
Go to the Keyword Planner homepage using the tutorial above. Select on the first option, "Search for new keyword and ad group ideas". In the dropdown menu, it will give you three options. Go to the second option which allows you to input a URL.

CHAPTER 1: KEYWORD RESEARCH

In this section, input one of the following URL's:
- **Pinterest Boards** – Search on Pinterest for your keyword, eg: "making soap" and get the URL for one of the boards.
- **Blog Posts** – Do a search on Google for your desired keyword and copy the URL of a popular, high traffic blog post.
- **BuzzSumo** – This site shows you the most shared content in your niche. Input your niche (eg: makeup) and copy the links of the first few results.

By inputting a URL, the tool will show you all the keywords that are directing traffic to that site. These keywords are usually hidden from public view, but they are yours to enjoy!

17. Get Visual Data On Long Tail Keywords
Need some long tail keywords? This tool will give you a very unique perspective on long tail keyword research. Simply type in the start of a question such as "why am i" or "why doesn't she" and you'll see the innermost thoughts that people have. Results such as "why am I single", "why is she avoiding me" and "why is she wearing leggings" crop up, as well as search volumes and competition for those questions.

It's not the best keyword tool, but it is quirky and makes research a little more interesting!
Play around with it, and you'll discover some very interesting insights into the minds of the public. (www.hint.fm/seer)

18. Get Commonly Asked Questions/Statements/Long Tail Keywords
This is yet another tool I have discovered on my travels. It's called Answer The Public (www.answerthepublic.com) and it basically provides an entire list of questions which people have asked on Google. You type in a broad keyword such as "dresses" or "cars" and this tool will generate over one hundred questions related to that keyword such as "how dresses changed over the years", "what dresses to wear in winter" or "where to buy dresses in Toronto".

It will also generate over hundred statements about that topic such as "dresses with short sleeves", "dresses which suit short hair" or "prom dresses near me".

This tool is amazing, there's no other way to say it. The best part about it is that it generates the questions in a visual "wheel", and it's quite a sight.

For some long tail keywords and frequently asked questions, you won't find a better tool.

19. Get Keywords From Your Friends and Colleagues
With the shift to Google Hummingbird and keywords becoming more conversational, it's a great idea to get keyword suggestions from your friends and colleagues. They can provide you with more ideas and suggestions than any keyword tool.

The best way to do this is with a new tool which can be found at www.seedkeywords.com. This tool allows you to input a "scenario" such as "What would you search for on Google, if you wanted ideas for Christmas gifts?". The tool will generate a unique URL to this scenario, which you can send to your friends and colleagues at work. By clicking the link, they will be asked what keywords they would type into Google for that topic. You can then analyze the keywords and see how they fare in terms of traffic with the Google Keyword Planner!

It's a quick and easy way to get more keyword ideas from your friends, family and colleagues, without annoying them!

20. Keyword Eye
Get a wildly different perspective on keyword research! This uses imagery (size and colour) to illustrate keyword data. Enter a keyword into the tool and it'll generate tens of keywords in a "word cloud" style. Bigger keywords have more monthly searches whilst the competition of each keyword is illustrated by a colour.

Red is for high competition, yellow for medium and green for low competition. It's perfect when searching for new ideas and always leads to that "creative spark". It's quite a refreshing way to do keyword research!

21. MetaGlossary.com

This website is a real treat. It is not a keyword tool at all but a dictionary. It provides definitions for words but also displays "similar words" along with them. You can get more than a hundred "related words" per keyword that you input. Eg: Search for the word "SEO" on the tool.

You'll get a pile of definitions for what it means but at the top of the page, there are more than one hundred SEO-related terms! Many tools just spew out closely related terms but this understands the actual meaning behind the word. For example, "spamdexing", "crawling" and "keyword research" are included on the list. Copy all these words and get analyzing!

22. Access Over A Trillion Keywords at Wordstream

Get a boatload of new keywords with Wordstream. With over a trillion keywords in their database, you're bound to find some very profitable keywords indeed. I just wish I knew about this sooner. It's free too, meaning you don't have to spend lots of money on keyword research. (www.wordstream.com)

23. Google Trends

The homepage displays trending searches in the past few hours. If you want a publicity boost, you can write on a trending search term. Check out the top ten trending keywords and see if you can write on any. You can also search for your targeted keywords and see if they are popular today.

You will be shown a graph on the popularity of your keyword over time, and what its predicted forecast might be. The tool will generate some new keywords at the bottom of the page too, giving some extra ideas.

24. Forums Contain Keyword Gold

Take a scroll through forums and QA sites and you'll see that the questions people ask can easily be turned into keywords you can research. If someone's asking it, chances are, hundreds of others are probably wondering what the answer/solution is too. Check our QA sites such as Yahoo! Answers and Quora. Also, check out forums such as Reddit and search for forums in your niche using this search string: "[niche] forum".

Search for questions on the forum and statements that are being brought up on the forum. Try to turn these into keywords, and analyse them using the GKP!

25. Get The Keywords That Are Sending Traffic To Your Competitors
What keywords are sending the most traffic to your competitors? You'd be very surprised.

With SpyFu (www.spyfu.com), you get access to the hottest keywords that are sending traffic to your competitors. You also get insights on the amount of clicks that those keywords are bringing to the website, which is a very rare metric to get.

You also get access to the most profitable ads that they have been putting up on Google AdWords. This is great because you can see what keywords have been generating them the most clicks. It's often a waste of money doing "experiments" (which ad gets more clicks, A or B?) on Google AdWords or testing which ad is most effective. With this tool, you get the results to the experiments your competitors have been doing immediately.

SpyFu offers an incredibly vast amount of information on the keywords you're competitors are using. It's probably one of my favourites and whenever I need some ideas, I also head over to it.

26. Use Google Wild Card Suggest
Google have their own wild card operator which means you can generate words. You may have used Google Autosuggest find more keywords to target. However, the suggested words don't appear until the end of the phrase. With the wild card operator, Google will suggest random yet frequently searched words to replace the wild card operator. In other words, a Google Autosuggest search may yield something like, "books for teens". If you placed a wild card operator in the phrase, "_ books for kids", you would get phrases such as "**best** books for kids", "**nonfiction** books for kids", "**colouring books** for kids" appear.

The wild card operator is denoted by an underscore (_) or an asterisk (*). Very few know of this tactic so use it to your advantage!

27. Get Keywords That'll Be Massively Searched For In The Future

It's time to have a massive opportunity over everyone else. Get out your crystal ball and start looking for keywords that will be searched for massively in the future. Since it takes about three months for a webpage's SEO work to kick in, you can start early by ranking for future keywords now.

Type dates after your keyword, such as "marketing 2016" or "Christmas men's gifts 2016". Really, all you need is your niche followed by the year. People are going to be searching for these keywords in their thousands (or millions) when the time comes, so be the first and seize the opportunity. As the saying goes, the early bird catches the worm.

Also, focus on highly anticipated product launches which are going to take place a few months or even a year from now. For example, "apple watch launch" or "google glass launch".

28. Go Local

If you have a local business, it would be foolish not to go for keywords aimed at your local area. Instead of trying to rank for "gardening center" would be absolutely impossible to rank for on page one. Instead, try ranking for keywords such as "garden center Bristol". Take the size of the area into account too.

Keywords such as "gardening center arizona" would be more difficult to rank for than "gardening center phoenix". Again, check search volume for the smaller town, larger city or area (province, state, county) and see which is most profitable and has the least competition.

29. Get "Urgency Keywords"

People that search for things like "flower delivery same day" or "Valentine's gifts next day" are more likely to buy something since they need something fast. These keywords emit a sense of urgency so you can cash in by providing a same day delivery. You can prepare for this by including "same day" or "next day" in your keywords if you are an online business.

30. Get "Spammy" Keywords

These keywords promise things that don't exist such as "how to grow hair in one week", "rank website in 24 hours" or "lose two stone in one day". Trying to propose these is simply nonsense and searching for any of these results in a lot of spammy, poor quality websites ranking. You know those online ads you see that propose a "weird tip that you can use to lose weight"? Those websites usually are nothing more than scams.

However, you can create an excellent piece of content which legitimately helps people with their problem. Start off by saying that such an idea is impossible, and then, offer alternatives instead. For example, say that trying to grow back your hair in one week is never going to happen but there are other measures you can take to get your hair growing back in a month. It might not answer their specific query, but it's a whole lot better than paying a visit to those scam websites!
Since your article is of a very high quality, it's going to rank first because all the other websites are spam (which we all know Google hates).

It's important not to choose overly spammy keywords (like "payday loans" for example) because they'll only ring alarm bells for Google. Keep topics on the safe side, and don't go overboard on this strategy!

31. Targeting An Older Audience? Use Bing

If you are in a niche that has an older, less tech savvy audience - you may need to focus on keywords which can be found on Bing. Go to the Bing Keyword Planner at http://www.bing.com/toolbox/keywords and search for your desired keywords.

32. Don't Place Your Keywords Into The Meta Keywords Tag

Once you have a keyword list that you want to target, do not place it into the meta keywords tag. Google doesn't value this HTML tag anymore and it's just way for competitors to see what keywords you're targeting which means a lot of stolen keywords. A lot of old school SEO websites still recommend the meta keywords tag, but Google stopped placing value on it six years ago. There's no point trying to make that tag work now.

How To Embed Keywords Into Your Content For Best Rankings

33. Use Your Keywords Through Creating Webpages or Content
Once you find keywords you need to make them *work* for you. That means, bringing customers, leads and ultimately, revenue to you and your website.

You need to create either webpages or content surrounding the keywords that you've picked. If you are a local business wanting to get more traffic to your website (from those keywords), you need to make webpages about your business and what you offer to customers using the keywords in the title. For example, if you provide web design services to clients in London, you're keywords would be "web design London" and you're homepage title could be something like, "Web Design In London: Making Beautiful Websites Since 2007". You would then place the keywords in the relevant places as mentioned below.

Once you have an initial set of webpages, you can then start creating content targeting other keywords that you have found. Content can take in the form of a blog post, infographic or video – and usually solves or answers the problems that are in your niche, eg: "how to be a successful author" would be a good keyword for someone to target that offers marketing for authors.

34. Place Your Keywords In Relevant Places
For a fully optimized page, adding keywords in the right places is essential. You need to have a special keyword in mind when creating your content. By targeting a certain keyword phrase, and placing it in the relevant areas, you are telling Google that your content is about [your keyword] in a sure-fire and clear way, meaning it's relevant.

When you don't really know what you're targeting, you probably have everything all over the place, giving little results. By knowing the keyword you are targeting, you can analyze the page's position in the rankings, crush any competition you have and more. There are 5 exact areas to drill your keywords in.

1. **Title (H1 Tag)** – With keywords, Google puts the most weight on the Title Tag. In HTML speak, it's known as the H1 Tag. Make sure that the keyword is clearly in the title. Make sure your title is no more than 65 characters, or else it will be chopped off in both search results and on social media.

2. **URL** – Make sure to only include the keyword phrase you are targeting in the URL. Don't keep unnecessary words such as "and", "a" or "guide". I have found that including just the keywords in the URL tend to be valued more by Google. The URL can always be different to the title of the content, so keep URL length to a minimum.

3. **Meta Description** – This is the summary of your article (appears on Google rankings) which gives you an overview on what the content is actually about. Google don't **value the keywords** in this. The description is merely used to grab people's attention and clinch the click. An effective description should pose a question, add juicy promises and get people excited about what the page has to offer. Keep sentences short and to the point. Lead off the summary with an ellipsis "…" to make people curious and click to read more. Here's an example:

> "Learn how to make pink lemonade, in this illustrated guide! Get all the tips and tricks for a juicy and refreshing drink. This lemonade is so good that…"

The words underlined appeal to the desires of people and make them want to read more. My article has tips and tricks (some exclusivity there!) and offers an illustrated guide. The ellipsis leads to a little mystery, who knows what's next? Stay within 160 characters, or else it will be chopped off.

4. **First 100 Words** – In the actual article itself, Google focus a little more on the first 100 words than everything else, so make sure that you insert the keyword phrase you are targeting. This will officially pay tribute to what your title, subheadings and meta description are all about.

CHAPTER 1: KEYWORD RESEARCH

5. **Content** – When you write about the keywords, you will naturally include them in your content without even realizing it. When the Googlebots crawl your article, they don't actually crawl small, non-important words like "and", "the" or "a". Instead, they only crawl instances of keywords. For example, on an article about laptops, they would index "dell, "review of toshiba", "laptop accessories", "laptop extras" and so on. These words are taken into account when Google ranks you. Keep a constant focus on the keyword phrase you are targeting.

35. Place Targeted Keyword At Start of Title –
If possible, you should put the exact keyword or keyword phrase at the beginning of the title. Google have stated that titles with the keyword in the first 3-4 words do better than those without. So instead of "A Detailed Guide to Planting Tomato Seeds" you could say "Tomato Seeds: How To Plant".

36. Watch Out For Keyword Stuffing -
Some think that the more they insert keywords into content, the higher they'll rank. This technique is called **keyword stuffing.** It can end up pretty bad with webmasters including the keyword hundreds of times in their content.
That used to work in the past, (back in the darker, black hat days) but not anymore.
Keyword density is the amount of times your keyword appears in your content divided by the total number of words. So, if I used the phrase "make lemonade" twenty times and I wrote 1500 words, my keyword density would be 20 / 1500 x 100 = 1.33%.

You don't need to worry at all about keyword density. It's a thing of the past and is a very weak ranking factor. Just bear in mind that your targeted keyword shouldn't have a keyword density of over 3%. Anything more than that, and you are entering the danger zone.

37. Keyword Variations
You should add variations of your keyword throughout the content. You can find variations of keywords in Google's Related Searches box. Do a search of your target keyword on Google and scroll down to the Related Searches box. You should find plenty of variations of the keyword. Include these into your sub-headings and text for an added relevancy boost.

38. Want to Start Using Paid Keyword Tools?

The free tools that I have mentioned provide pretty much everything you need for keyword research from keyword generation to keyword analysis. All the tools that I've mentioned until now are completely free and will probably remain that way.

However, if you want to simplify the keyword process and make it faster, paid keyword tools might be an option for you. I'm not saying that you need paid tools but if you feel like you want to cut down the time you spend on keyword research, paid tools offer the advanced functionality that provides that.

For generating long tail keywords and their monthly Google searches, try out LongTail Pro. You need to input a single keyword such as "Italian cooking" or "keyword research" and it will generate hundreds of popular long tail keywords you can use immediately to start ranking. The free alternative would be Google Keyword Planner and Ubersuggest.

I would also recommend SEMRush (www.semrush.com), and Keyword Project Manager (www.keywordprojectmanager.com) which are amazing tools for keyword research.

CHAPTER 2
Competition Analysis

The sites that rank in the Google search results for a particular keyword are known as your *competition*. When hundreds of high authority websites rank for a particular keyword, there is a small chance you will too. These websites with a high PageRank and strong online presence are impossible to beat because they have strong PageRank, thousands of valuable backlinks and killer content. Once you have established yourself as an expert in your niche, by writing lots of content, you will have the credibility to take on some of these sites. But for now, you need to find keywords which have relatively low competition.

39. Competition Is Important
When lots of low authority websites rank for a traffic earning keyword, you've just hit the sweet spot. That means your website can bulldoze through the rankings to number one, and clinch all that sweet traffic.

If you select a keyword with thousands of monthly searches but has high competition, you will find it very difficult to break through the barrier. That's why doing some competition analysis is so important. By seeing what the competition is like, you can see how many backlinks you'll have to build to reach the top spot and what kind of content you'll need.

40. What is Competition Measured In?
Competition is measured by PageRank and Domain Authority. These two factors both tell you what the quality of the sites is and whether you should start targeting a keyword.

PageRank is the algorithm that made Google's search results so relevant and what made it stand apart from the other search engines. PageRank is a very complicated algorithm in practice, but it's easy enough to understand in theory. Every website, blog and page on the internet is assigned PageRank, which is on a scale from zero to ten.

Once your site becomes established, it will begin to receive backlinks from other websites. A backlink is an organic link to your page from another website. When you begin to get more of these links, your PageRank begins to increase.

The more quality links you have to your page, the higher your PageRank goes. When a website links to your website, it gives some of its PageRank to you. So if a dodgy forum site linked to your content and had a PR of zero, you would receive barely any PR at all (it would even damage your site's reputation).

But if Wikipedia, a university or government website linked to you and they had a PR of 6 or 7, then you would receive a lot of PageRank. Google still put much emphasis on PageRank even post-Panda. High authority pages have a higher PageRank and the beginning, mediocre websites have a small PageRank. PageRank is a small factor but it was the signal that made Google the company it is today.

That is why you should check the PageRank of the top 10 search results for your targeted keywords. You can then make a judgment on whether competition is too high or easy game.

Domain Authority is on a scale of 1 to 100. This takes content quality, links, social shares and influence into account. High quality websites with lots authoritative content and tons of good backlinks have a higher DA than low quality websites.

41. How To Analyze Your Competition Easily (PageRank)

You can check both the PageRank and Domain Authority of your competition using tools such as prchecker.net and opensiteexplorer.com. However, with these – you can only check one website at a time. When you want to check more than ten sites at once, you will need a tool to do it for you.

The best tool for this is *Niche Market Finder* (http://www.seodevgroup.com/products/niche-market-finder.html).

CHAPTER 2: COMPETITION ANALYSIS

You can use Niche Market Finder to quickly analyze the competition for a certain search phrase or keyword. When you input a keyword, the tool will find all the pages that rank for that keyword. Their PageRank and other details are looked at. It is a quick and fast way to seeing what the competition is like.

Once you have it downloaded, open it up and take a look at it, just to get a feel for it.

Type in your keyword into the search box and press, "Find Pages". A list of all the pages will appear and you can see what PR your competitors have. Pages with a PR of 4 or more will be very difficult to rank alongside if you have a starting website. Pages from 1 to 3 are a lot easier to rank with.

Target keywords that have lower PageRank (0-3) websites in search results.

42. A Quick Overview On The Types Of Competition

Once you have some Niche Market Finer results loaded up, start checking the results out using this guide. Here is a scale you can use to assess the playing field based on the PageRank of your competition.

- **Very Low Competition (Moneymaker):** This typically includes websites with low PR's (0,1,2) and poor content (less than 700 words). Lots of fantastic content and a couple of backlinks are the formula to taking these guys down.
- **Medium Competition (First Pager):** These rankings have a mix of high and low PR websites in the 0-5 range. They have a variety of high and medium quality content. Some will have some very obvious SEO done, whilst others have a poor attempt at it. You may not get the first spot in these rankings too easily, but middle of the first page is a safe bet.
- **High Competition (Tough Cookie):** Here, you will find websites that know their stuff with PR's in the 3-5 range. Spots are reserved for well-known websites and experts in the field. After building up your blog and getting it popular and well-known, you can target a place here but it will take a lot of work. In the end, it pays off because keywords with this competition usually get tens of thousands of searches a month.

- **Extremely High Competition (Warzone):** I hate to break it to you but if Wikipedia, MSN, YouTube or high PR websites are ranking for over five results, your website won't have a single chance. These websites have a soaring PageRank and when I say high, I mean high. Wikipedia's PR is 9, YouTube's is 9 and MSN's is 8. Even with a website with $20,000+ SEO work and a PR of 5, you still cannot get past them.

30. Check Your Competitor's Keywords

Keywords play a huge part in competition too. If you contain the exact keyword phrase in your Title Tag, Google will value your page higher than others with variations of the keyword. That's why you need to see how many of the pages target that exact keyword phrase. If every page has the exact keyword phrase in its title tag, your competition will be higher. Whereas, if some of the pages have the exact keyword and others have variations, your page will be valued higher for that keyword.

For example, a page titled, "How To Make Great Lemonade" will rank higher for the search phrase "great lemonade" rather than "How To Make Lemonade With A Twist".

43. Watch Out For Exact Match Domains

Are there any exact match domains? These are domains which target a precise keyword of keyword phrase. If thousands of people search for a certain keyword phrase, you can create a website with that exact keyword phrase as your URL. Google have always given them more advantage in search results, eg: www.typesofinsects.com would target the exact keyword phrase "types of insects".

Before, Google always gave these exact match domains the first or second spot simply because their URL included the exact keyword, even if their website was bogus. After the EMD update, if a website's content is not high quality, its EMD status would disappear.

If you see an EMD in the rankings you are targeting, check it out and answer these questions. Does the site look genuine by having no affiliate links, heavy advertising or poor copy? Does it have a fluent site design? Does it have a blog which produces amazing content? If you answered yes to all three of these, you are going to have a hard time blasting this website off the rankings. If not, your quality will beat what they have.

44. For Content: Check Out The Top Content
When checking out your competition's content (as in, blog posts or articles), try and answer the following questions:
Does it have more than three attributed images?
Does it have more than 1500 words?
Is it engaging, and easy to read?
Is the page delivering a good user experience?

Answering yes to all of these questions means that you will have to step it up a gear in terms of content. That means more words, images and videos. It means creating engaging and interactive material that is clear and concise.

45. Use SEOQuake: Another Competition Analysis Tool
An extremely valuable tool that checks your competition in search rankings is called SEOQuake. You simply search one of your targeted keywords and it displays a toolbar underneath each result. This toolbar displays factors such as number of backlinks, age and PageRank. This makes it easy to see if you can match with your competitors' achievements.

You should focus a lot more on PageRank because it is a much more accurate way of getting a "count" or measure of backlinks and their quality. SEOQuake displays PageRank too throughout each result so you can see if they are beatable.

To use SEOQuake you will need either Google Chrome or Mozilla Firefox as a browser. Internet Explorer isn't being catered for at the moment so make sure to download a suitable browser. We will be using these browsers again soon for other tools, so the download is worth it.

After you have a browser installed, it's time to download SEOQuake. Go to www.seoquake.com and download it for your browser. For Chrome, you can get it up and running by going to the "Toolbar" section of your browser and choosing "Extensions". You can then click on SEOQuake's extension and then click to enable it.

46. Watch Out For "Easy To Beat Websites" - If you see any of these websites ranking, you know that you can beat them with a little work. Here is a list of common easy to beat websites that you can easily outsmart.

- **Amazon/Sales Pages** –No one really likes long lists of products and neither does Google. Should you find any product listings standing boldly in your way – you can beat them.
- **Unregistered Domains** – These are usually websites that have a free domain name such as www.myweb.weebly.com or www.myweb.blogspot.com. The reason they are easy to beat is because the owners probably wanted to become "a well-known blogger", wrote a few posts (with no SEO or social media optimization), realized no one cares and left. These thin, five post blogs have no authority and so, you can easily get past them.
- **HubPages, InfoBarrel or Ezine Articles** – These are article directories, which have thousands of authors to write articles for them. Most of their articles are poor quality and they aren't in the good books at the moment. Google have publicly announced that war is on content farms, so your content should beat them with some SEO and great quality stuff.

47. Browse Incognito To Get Un-Personalized Search Results
When you are checking what your competition is like on Google for certain keywords (especially for local searches), your search results will be personalized. There could be outside factors which influence your results, such as location, device and previous browsing history.

To get rid of the personalization of search, open an Incognito Window in Google Chrome, or "Private Page" in Mozilla Firefox. These windows don't use cookies, extra data or previous browsing history to influence your search results.

You basically start off on a clean slate, you're an anonymous internet user and the results you get are not personalized.

However, I must note that there can still be a certain degree of personalization such as your location. Still, the degree of personalization is not as pronounced as in a regular search results page.

48. Add "pws=0" To Remove Personalization
By adding this parameter to the Google search URL, you are telling Google not to personalize the search result. Combine this with the step above and you will "de-personalize" your search result as much as possible.

Type the following into your browser address bar, where your desired keyword follows after the "q=".
www.google.com/?q=seo&pws=0

49. Make Sure You're Signed Out of Google, For No Personalization
This is very important! If you don't sign out of your Google Account, performing the two steps above won't yield any results.
You will know if you're signed into Google, by checking if your email or Google+ profile is listed in the top right corner of Google Search.

50. Don't Measure Competition Through The Number of Search Results
A lot of webmasters say that the more results a topic has, the more difficult it is to rank on page one or even page two for that matter. So, if one keyword has 4,780,000 search results and another has 250,000 – it is assumed automatically that it's a whole lot easier to rank for the second keyword, right? You'd assume so. I would too.

However, the strength of the pages (in other words, PageRank and Domain Authority) ranking for the second keyword could be very high, meaning you'd never have a chance of ranking.
Whilst the number of pages can be a vague indicator, it still doesn't tell you the strength of those pages or how good their content is. Don't really take this into huge consideration when you're analysing competition of certain keywords, check the PageRank of the ranking pages first.

51. How To Check Competition In Certain Countries

If your target audience is outside of your country, you may need to do research in other countries or check Google rankings for other locations. However, you can't just type in www.google.de for the German Google search engine. You will be automatically redirected back to your country's Google search engine. However, there are two ways to do bypass this annoying redirect.

A Good Ol' Google Search

Just type the country's Google address into your browser, and type "ncr" after the URL which stands for "No Country Redirect". If you type www.google.de into your browser, your browser will automatically redirect you to the google address for your countrye, eg: if you were living in the US and typed www.google.co.uk into your browser, you would be redirected to www.google.com.

So, type the following into your browser address bar, www.google.co.uk/ncr and you will be able to access the Google UK page. Now, you can check for what sites are ranking for keywords, in various countries.

Automate The Process With RankTracker

RankTracker is a free tool which allows you to check the rankings of your website for certain keywords in various countries. If you'd rather have the task of checking rankings in other countries become automated, this is the tool for you. Download RankTracker at www.link-assistant.com/rank-tracker

CHAPTER 3
On-Page SEO

On-page SEO is all about optimizing your page so that Google knows what keywords you want to rank for. It's also about making sure that you have the right elements on-page, so that you will keep both your readers and Google happy. A strategic, easy to read page lays a powerful foundation for heading into the rankings.

Optimizing The URL

52. Include Only Targeted Keywords In The URL
Include your targeted keywords in the URL. This will specifically tell Google what your page is exactly about…no questions asked. It would also give your page an immediate boost in the rankings, because it is so targeted at that keyword phrase.

53. Keep The URL Short
Keep the URL under 100 characters. Any longer than that, and things start to get a little messy. Preferably, you should keep your URL under 50 characters to be more suitable for social sharing, bookmarks, email links and so on. When people see a short URL, they are more likely to share it on social media since it's short, tells their followers what the page is about and doesn't clog up the social media post. Compare this to using a shortened link such as a bit.ly link. Since it doesn't actually tell you what the domain is, people would be more reluctant to click on it.

54. Hierarchy's In A URL Show Extra Relevance
Your website may be divided up into a hierarchy. Pages may be organized under several category pages, eg: technical SEO or keyword research. For example, if you wrote a page about Vitamin C benefits and placed it into the "vitamins" category, your URL would look like this:
www.yourdomain.com/vitamins/vitamin-c-benefits
Hierarchy's can give extra details to Googlebots that display more relevance.

55. Don't Overdo Folders In Your URLs

It's good practice to place blog posts into their relevant folders, but don't include more than one folder (two folders max) in your URL. Any more than that, and the user starts to get detracted from the whole purpose of the URL which is, telling the user what kind of a page they'll be landing on. For example:

www.website.com/business-and-finance/finance/personal-finance/money-saving-tips

This URL contains way too many folders and only junks up the entire URL. Instead, shorten it down to something like this:

www.website.com/finance/personal-finance/money-saving-tips

Or even better, try this:

www.website.com/personal-finance/money-saving-tips

56. Get Rid of Unnecessary Words In The URL

Take out any unnecessary words that don't have any impact on the meaning of the URL Avoid any flabby words such as "the", "a", "in", "or" "and". They aren't counted for anything really - and puff up your URL to a much longer size.

57. Separate URLs with Hyphens/Underscores, Not Spaces

Yeah. Believe me, I've seen URLs that had spaces separating the words. Don't try it, because it causes all kinds of issues with search engines and hosting services.

58. Don't Keyword Stuff Your URLs

It's still a common sight to see URLs that contain their targeted keyword phrase more than once. For example, www.website.com/cute-puppies-10-pics-of-cute-puppies. Whilst you may be tempted to get a relevancy boost by including your keyword twice, don't even think about doing it. This practice is old school and you'll only get penalized for it.

Essential On-Page Elements To Add

59. Make Sure You've Included Your Keywords
Google isn't psychic, it doesn't know if you want to rank for a certain keyword (well, not yet). You need to tell it specifically what keywords you want to rank for.

The best way to do this is to place your keywords into your title tag, first 100 words, content and sub-headings. However, don't overdo this as it can get risky!

60. Links To Authority Websites
Google have actually stated that when you link to authority websites (Wikipedia or .edu sites, for example) you may get an increase in PageRank. This is because it signifies relevance and quality. If you chose to link to Wikipedia, it must mean that you want only the best content for your readers.

Even two links in your content is sufficient to show that you have linked back to further research. Think about it. Would you prefer linking to a shoddy affiliate site than someone linking to an article by Harvard? Thought so.

This little technique is not well known in the SEO community so use this trick to your advantage.

61. Awesome Content
So what kind of content does Google love and how can you best go about that? The answer is *quality*. I never liked people harping on about something but if there is something to harp on about, this is it.
I think it's time to start realizing the effects that stunning content is having on Google. Even without any SEO (just targeting a certain keyword), it is still possible to rank on page one for medium competition terms!

Most people don't have a clue about what SEO is and can still rank on page one for keywords they tried to target. It's the off-page strategies that get you ranking *first* for those terms.

The side-effects of great content not only applies to SEO but to social media sharing and building backlinks. When you create a piece of content that just knocks everything else out of the water, you have a **right** to get this shared across the web.

Here's a quick overview on what "quality" defines:
1. **1500+ Words** – Google knows the quality when they see the length. Would you rank a 700 word article higher than a 1700 word article? Thought not.
2. **Images** – Whilst you may not get much traffic from Google Images, incorporating imagery into your content is another quality signal to Google. If they are original (not from stock photo) sites, this is even better.
3. **Video and other Multimedia** – Videos and other multimedia, reduce your bounce rate and increase page dwell time. This produces engagement and a better user experience for every searcher.
4. **Sub-headings** – Nobody likes boring blocks of text all piled up into one mass mess. By having relevant (and keyword-rich) sub-headings in your content, you can target long tail keywords and break up the monotony that lots of text brings.

62. Don't Banish The Meta Description Just Because It Isn't A Ranking Factor

Meta descriptions are the little snippet of text that goes underneath the blue link in search results. Google have stated on their blog that the meta description is not a ranking factor, and that the keywords in the meta description will not be factored into the search algorithm.

This led many webmasters to believe that meta descriptions are useless, a complete waste of time and should be banished from their SEO efforts altogether.

But that's like committing digital suicide. You couldn't go more astray from the reality.

Meta descriptions are you're only point of contact with the customer. You need to sell your message to them. Your meta description has to be the best, and attract more eyeballs than anyone else's.

Google *do* take Click Through Rates (percentage of searchers that click on your result, over anyone else's, if 3 out of 10 searchers clicked on my link, my CTR would be 30%) into consideration when ranking your page. If your search result is enticing, and leads to a high CTR – your website must be useful and relevant to searchers. The only way to make your search result enticing and attractive is to have a click worthy title, tempting meta description and some rich snippets if you have the chance to use them.

The main point to take away from this is that you need a meta description, and even though some SEO experts may warn against them – always make the meta description the best that you can possibly make it.

63. Make Your Meta Description Alluring and Practical

Your meta description has to ignite curiosity within the searcher but also be practical at the same time. This contrast is the key to writing successful meta descriptions. In short, tell the reader what they'll find and then make them want more.

Be Practical
- Include your targeted keywords. This will make them bold so that when a searcher looks for those keywords on Google, they will see the bold words meaning relevance. When most of your competitors will have the search query in bold, you'd be foolish not to include the keyword.
- Give a quick overview of what the page is about.

Be Tempting
- Make the user curious by cutting your meta description off with an ellipsis (…) at the end.
- Offer juicy promises and be bold.
- Make them want more information.

Fuse the two together, and you get a masterpiece of a meta description.

Technical Details
- Take out quotation marks, Google will cut them out.
- Keep your meta description between 150-160 characters, to avoid it getting chopped off.
- Don't use the same meta description in multiple pages. You risk getting it caught as a piece of duplicate content, so watch it.

64. Use These Meta Description Templates
If you need some quick inspiration before you get working on your meta descriptions, take a look at these. The first is for an online business and the other two are for blog posts.

Want a compelling logo design for your company? At LogoCompany, we provide professional logos at great prices. Get a 50% discount when you order a logo today.

Want more traffic? Learn how to get more traffic today with these 20 simple SEO tricks, that you've probably never seen before. These tricks will give you results in days!

Learn how to create delicious cheesecake with this recipe (featured on the Rachel Ray show) With step by step instructions, images and top tips.

65. Optimize Your Meta Description Using AdWords
If you take a look at some of the meta descriptions that AdWords ads are using, you can get keywords which are guaranteed to get clicks.

For example, let's say you're selling pillows and you want to get as many clicks to your website as possible. Some of the AdWords ads contain the words, "free delivery", "wide range", "soft or firm pillows" and so on. You can include all these words together, leading to an unbeatable meta description!
"Browse through a <u>wide range</u> of pillows, including <u>soft or firm pillows</u>. Plus, get <u>free delivery</u> internationally. Find the pillow of your dreams now!"

66. Cut Bounce Rate Through Internal Linking
Bounce rate is the number of people that leave your site without progressing further into the site. You need to keep users on your site, and slash your bounce rate. Bounce rate is a very important ranking factor to Google – because a high bounce rate website indicates that something is a little dodgy. For example, if you clicked on a website that had "pay $1500 to access material NOW!" plastered all over the page, in flashing red – you'd click back out in an instant, with your heart palpitating. It looks strange if every visitor left your site immediately after clicking in.

Cut your bounce rate by creating compelling content on a well-designed website. Also, link to related articles of yours at least once in your text. This will pass some PageRank to your site, cut bounce rate and get more readers

67. Google Authorship No Longer Exists
A lot of blog posts haven't been updated yet and still contain outdated information. If you've read that you should join Google Authorship or link your Google+ profile to your blog posts, just remember that Google removed this feature over six months ago. If you don't know what Authorship was, you've probably seen it before. Remember when search results were accompanied by a profile picture and a by-line? That was Google Authorship.

A lot of tutorials and SEO guides still recommend joining Google Authorship but remember that it's no longer possible for now.

68. Social Sharing Buttons Are Essential
Whilst social media signals are very weak ranking factors right now, I think that they will become more important in the future.
Looking at it from a non-SEO perspective, social media can supplement your traffic just in case your rankings change.

Place social sharing buttons in a prominent position such as on the side of the page, at the bottom, on the top or both. You can add a "call to action" at the end of the page. A call to action is basically a phrase that encourages people to share your content or to buy something. For example, *"Share today to let everyone know of this!"*.

69. Rich Snippets/Schema Markup
Rich snippets are extra "add-ons" you can apply to your search result listing such as review stars, recipe times, location, images, calories, number of votes and publish date.

The advantage of using rich snippets is that they increase the amount of searchers who click on your link. Including stars, calories and a splat of colour deeply enhance your pitch to the searcher. It is a fact that including rich snippets in your page increases Click Through Rate by 20-30%. Make sure that rich snippets are part of your on-page SEO.

70. Get Rich Snippets With These Tools

The first option is to use the Google Data Markup Highlighter. This tool can be found in Webmaster Tools. You simply paste in the URL you want to add schema markup in, fill in the details (number of review stars, number of minutes to make) and copy the HTML. It is a point and click tool, and is very easy to use.

The second tool you can use is www.schema-creator.org and is another excellent way to create rich snippets. You can use this to generate schema mark-up for any rich snippets you want to add. Simply fill in the details, copy the code and paste it into your website.

71. Check That Your Rich Snippets Are Working

Adding rich snippets to your site can go wrong very quickly, so always double check that they actually appear and are working properly.

The best way to do this is by going to Google's very own schema mark-up checker: www.developers.google.com/structured-data/testing-tool/ All you have to do is input your page's URL by clicking on the "Fetch as URL" button.

72. Use Review Stars, Calories and Time for Recipes and Tutorials

Make sure to use the full power of rich snippets by including them on every possible page. If you have content which teaches people how to do something make sure to get an advantage by including time and review stars on your page. Also, for recipes, include images and calories. The more, the merrier!

73. Keep An Eye On Technical Issues

Technical issues such as page load time, having a mobile website and indexing need to be attended to. Watch out for technical issues because if your technical issues aren't up to scratch, you could be losing out on higher rankings. Google take technical issues very seriously, and you need to make sure that all technical checks are performed on all your pages.

CHAPTER 3: ON-PAGE SEO

74. Include "Latent Semantic Indexing" Keywords, aka: synonyms
Latent Semantic Index keywords are words which are similar or found alongside your target keyword. For example, if your targeted keyword is "seo tips", some LSI keywords would be "keyword research", "on-page seo " and "technical seo". They're basically all words you'd expect to be in the content anyway.
Include variations of your keywords in your content, as the Hummingbird feeds off these. Google will then be able to "understand" what you're writing about, based on the LSI keywords you provide.

You can find LSI keywords in "Google's Relates Searches" box and also in Google Suggest. However, if you are writing quality content anyway, you will naturally be using LSI keywords anyway.

Image SEO

75. File Names Matter
Make sure that the names of the images you include are targeted towards your content, and not generic image names such as"DCIM331". If your blog post is about cooking pizza, an image called "pizza_ingredients" or "pizza_howto" would be very suitable. Google take image names into consideration when ranking your content, so always remember that!

76. Alt text
If your page fails to load properly, your images may not load either. Alt text basically describes what your image is about to search engines and users with low internet speed which results in their images not loading. Similarly, blind readers and those with disabilities can get the Alt text read to them. It helps a lot of people, and Google loves to see it too.

It might be an opportunity to slip in a keyword too, but don't add the keyword to every single image you have. That would be a bad, bad mistake.

77. Check Your Image SEO Automatically
Image SEO can become tedious especially when you have so many images to check. That's why you should automate it.

This tool checks the alt text of each image on the page you provide. It checks to see if the keywords conform to Google's quality guidelines and if they are an adequate length. It also checks the sizes of the images themselves, and make sure that they are of a suitable size. You will also find an astonishing number of other on-page SEO tools on the site. (www.feedthebot.com/alt)

CHAPTER 4

Linkbuilding

The more quality links your page gets, the higher your rankings will become. Once you have some content that's worthy of getting backlinks, you can start getting links by using the countless methods below. You'll learn practically every linkbuilding technique that exists or has existed. Also, don't worry – these linkbuilding techniques won't get your site penalized.

78. Linkbuilding Is Essential
Links are the currency of search engines. Linkbuilding is not dead. It never will be. Getting links show trust to Google, and give you a boost in PageRank. Aim for PR 2-4 links, as they provide the most value.
In short, links will raise your ranking in Google and get you to a higher spot for the keywords you are targeting.

Guest Posting Your Way To Fame And Success On The Web

79. What is guest posting?
Guest posting involves you writing a blog post for someone else who will publish this post on their blog. Instead of posting that content on your blog, it goes on someone else's blog or website and you do it for free. So what's the big deal? The positive with this tactic is that you can link to your site at least twice in the post. Guest posting is probably the easiest way to gain backlinks because it is simple to find blogs which are happy to publish your content.

The advantages of guest posting include the fact that:
- On high authority blogs, your site will get a ton of new readers who will get to know your brand/business/website or blog
- Your rankings on Google will increase
- More PageRank (especially from PR4-7 sites)
- Opportunities to work with bloggers in the future

80. There Are Two Types of Guest Posting, Watch Out

There are two kinds of guest posting which each make a huge impact on your blog. The first kind of guest posting is "guest posting for backlinks". Your focus is to get at least two high PR backlinks from this post and you don't care about actually getting any referral traffic from that site.

The second type is guest posting for promotion. Your aim here is *not* to get high PR backlinks but exposure. By writing on high power websites with huge audiences, your blog will get some exposure.

81. Find Blogs To Post On With Google Search

Believe it or not, you can actually search for blogs to write on without joining any guest blogging directories. It's simple. Identify whatever niche your blog focuses on, but keep it broad. Eg: fitness, science, cooking, machinery, DIY, children etc.

Then, perform the following Google searches. Fill in the [niche] with your own one. So, if my niche was technology, a search I would enter into Google is "technology write for us".

"[niche] write for us"
"[niche] guest posting"
"[niche] guest blog"

Alternatively, you can put in the name of a well-known person in your niche and find out where they have been guest posting.

"[person] guest post"

82. AllTop: Another Way To Find Blogs

Created by former Apple evangelist, Guy Kawasaki, this site showcases some of the best blogs in your niche. Simply go to www.alltop.com and select your niche from the dropdown menu. You will see a list of the most popular blogs in its category. Make note of these and search for all of them. Check whether or not these blogs allow guest posts or just contact them. See the template below for securing that guest post.

83. Find More Guest Posting Opportunities With MyBlogGuest

MyBlogGuest (www.myblogguest.com) allows you to find blogs that allow guest posting. You'll get all the specs and stats too, which is always handy. Sign up for an account and click into the category that your website belongs in. You will find multiple websites/blogs which allow guest posts. They will specify what PageRank their website is (most of the time) as well as good reasons why you should write for them. All kinds of specifications such as max. number of backlinks, word count, imagery and more are included along with the description.

This is a very useful resource for all website owners and bloggers because you get complete access to literally hundreds of domains that want guest posts. They are not only domains that accept guest posts but *want* them so they will be very grateful to have you!
It's like the Facebook of blogs and websites.

84. Check The Blog You Want To Post On First

The biggest mistake you could make when guest posting is writing on a blog that just isn't worth the time. There are millions out there to choose from so this means that you have all the leverage in this situation. When you start finding blogs to write on, remember to check the following factors:

- **PageRank** – A low PR (0-2) blog isn't worth it. There are thousands of high PR blogs to choose from, so don't go for the low PR blog.
- **Two Links** – How many links can you get? One link is too little, for all that effort. Two links is sufficient, and won't overpromote your website. Check with the blog/website owner before you submit your post to see how many links are allowed. Make sure that the links allowed are "dofollow" (Google will take this link into consideration when ranking) instead of "nofollow" (Link will not be counted as a backlink to your site).

85. Find Blogs That Pay You To Write For Them
Some blogs even *pay* you to write for them. It's a great way to get some promotion for your website, write about what you love and earn some cash in the process. Prices start from about $15 per blog post and can range up to $300 in some cases. Some blogs may not allow you to place a link in the post since they've paid you and expect no "promotion" in the article. Others may allow you to post a link in the Author Bio of your blog post. Keep an eye out for blogs that pay, because most of the time, you'll find it very difficult to actually place a link in your post.

86. Send Bloggers An Email
When contacting a blog for a guest post opportunity, you can use the template below if you wish.
Dear [Blog Owner Name],
I am a blogger who writes on [website URL] in the [your niche] area and I am a great fan of your blog. What useful resources for [blog's target audience]! I have written a blog post about [topic] and I would be thrilled if you could post it on your blog.
My blog post deals with [topic] and explores key ideas such as [topic]. As an online writer and social media expert, I think it will be a hit with your readers! Let me know if you are interested and I will send the post to you.
Thanks,
[Your Name]

87. How To Increase Your Chances Of Securing That Guest Post
There are several things you can do to make sure that you are accepted for a blog post. I've contacted tens of blogs every year for guest posts and found that the following strategies work:
- **Personalize Your Email**
- **Have A Nice Sounding Email Address** – Nothing signals spam more than a nonsensical email address filled with numbers, silly sounding words and other gibberish. If your email address is something like, 198gardeninginphoenix90l@youremailprovider.com you're going to have a hard time getting any replies back. For example, email such as phoenixgardencentre@email.com or

tim@gardencenter.com is a lot more professional sounding than the one above.
- **Have A Sample Of Your Writing Ready** – The best way to show them that you can write is by having a sample of your writing ready. Attach it to the email.
- **Be professional and witty at the same time**
- **Give an outline of what the post would cover**
- **Give a few reasons why your suited to the job**
- **Mention any social media profiles you have, any reports/books you've written or anything else that will help establish your credibility**

88. Offer To Write Them A Sequel To One of Their Posts
Are there any blog posts which have done extremely well on their blog? Try and see if you can make a sequel to that blog post. Since the blog post was very successful, there is no reason why your sequel shouldn't be equally as successful, if not better. It's foolproof. By rejecting you, they just lost a boatload of traffic which they could have got for free. They're saying no to free traffic.

It can be difficult to think of a sequel, but get your creative juices flowing. For example, the sequel after "How To Make Drizzled Lemon Cake" could be "3 Lemon Cake Recipes With A Unique Twist". Basically, advance from the last post by coming with a USP/unique selling point (I know it's a business term, but it works for SEO too. Right?) and advancing the idea further on.

89. Use The "Blank Post" Technique – Rarely, it's better not to mention the titles you want to write about such as if you get a rejection from them or can't think of any titles. You can use the "blank post" technique instead. This means that in your email, you should ask them if there is anything that they are thinking of writing, or any specific post they want written. If a blogger turns down your titles or ideas, try the blank post technique instead.

For example this snippet would be included in your email, *"Before I start mentioning titles, I just wanted to know if there is any topics you'd like more content on or if there's any ideas you thought would work. Let me know, and I'll write those blog posts for you."*

Who'd turn you down with a strong offer like that?

Getting Links On Resource/Sales Pages

90. Testimonials
Enjoy a product or service? Most companies offer you with the chance to provide a comment or personal experience on their "Testimonials" page. It's even better when you have a website (which you do) so at least you have some authority. Companies love linking back to the person who gave the testimonial because it gives more "reality" or realism to the actual comments. A headshot of yourself should also be included, but that is optional.

91. Join The "What the Press Say" Page
You will see that on many company websites, they will have a "What the Press Say" page. This is different from a testimonials page because the reviews come from websites, review sites and the blogging community rather than everyday people who don't have websites.
You can find out if there are any companies in your niche who have these pages by searching the following strings on Google:
"[niche] what the press say"
"[company] press"
You should find a couple of websites with these pages that are in your niche.
Write an in-depth and high quality review of your favorite product by this company and post it on your blog. Then, head over to the company's contact page and send them an email saying that you have written a review about their products and you would appreciate if it was put on their press page.

Most companies are happy to put your review on their page since the more positive reviews they have, the more customers will buy. However, others can be a little strict on what they allow. They may only consider your website should it have an audience, search traffic and about fifty to one hundred posts. To avoid this, build up your blog with plenty of in-depth posts and make them social media friendly (more on this in coming chapters) before approaching high end companies.
Build up your brand by guest blogging in your niche and having an active social media profile.

92. Link Requests
Sounds desperate right?
Think about it: Your aim as a website or blog is to create content which people will enjoy. Let's say a fellow writer says they read your article on X and they also wrote something related to X. You check out their content and it blew your socks off. You realize how much value it would provide to your reader. Wouldn't you link to it?

Most bloggers receive countless link requests and by now, they are probably tired of anything to do with links. But send them a request and you might get lucky.

93. Library Resource Pages
Libraries have resource pages on their websites which link to all kinds of articles, guides, tools and apps. They are always on the lookout for new guides to list on their resource pages, so if you have a resource such as an ultimate guide, short ebook or a research article, contact the library and you could get lucky. The links from a library's resource page are worth a lot and are considered of a very high quality.
"library [local area] resources"
"resources [name of library in your area]"

94. How To Get .edu Links
One link from a university website (eg: www.harvard.edu) and your website is set for life. University or faculty websites have a PageRank of 7, 8 and 9. Getting onto Harvard's homepage is pretty much impossible. Getting onto any of their pages is pretty much impossible, too.
However, most university websites have resource pages or "Further Links/References" pages which give internet links, documents and other kinds of goodies to students. They can read more about a topic, get more information on a certain aspect of the course or check out learning materials available on the web.

These pages have a PR of 4, 5 and 6 so getting your content on it will prove life-changing in terms of link juice.

Getting links from university websites doesn't necessarily mean that you need to write on "academic" subjects such as the sciences, literature or health. To find these resource pages, type the following search strings in to Google:
"site:.edu [your niche] resources"
"site:.edu [your niche] further reading"
"site:.edu [your niche] web links"
Take a look at some of the pages and see what kind of resources they link to. Are these pages high quality, with original imagery or are they mediocre? Can you do better?
If you can create a very useful resource page with at least 10 original images, personal experiences and some statistics, you can really appeal to a faculty.

Simply head over to the contact page of that specific department or get the contact email of the professor in that department. You can send them an email asking them to include your link on their page as it would greatly help students in their learning. If they are a local university and you live in their vicinity, your response rate will be even higher. Or, if you know a student going to university, you can ask them to recommend your resource (and that it greatly aided them in their studies!) to their professor who edits the department website.

Simple But Extremely Effective Tactics To Get High Value Links From Fellow Bloggers and Niche Influencers

95. Contact The Right Person For Outreach
Remember that when you are sending an outreach email (link requests, guest posts or broken link building), you need to send it to the right email. Many companies have a general email (eg: help@company.com) where you have to send an email to that address. However, make sure you contact the right person for outreach. Do some digging around the site before you just go and contact the general email.

Look for the person's email that's in charge of the blog, or a special email for guest post submissions. A simple thing like this could really speed up the time it takes to reach the right person, and make sure it actually gets read.

96. If You Have A Service/Online Course/Product/Ebook, Give To Bloggers For Free

Bloggers LOVE receiving a free product from a company, because it gives them some content to write about and also, they get a very valuable product for free. Many bloggers have a huge audience or email list and so, getting a review from them will result in a lot of exposure. Some bloggers focus on products only whilst others focus on specific niches such as cooking or technology.

97. Try Tomoson To Get Links From Bloggers

Tomoson (www.tomoson.com) is a service which connects bloggers with companies who offer products for free, in exchange for a review of their product (and a link). If you have any products you'd like to offer them, you can create a promotion on Tomoson. As soon as you post it, you'll get bloggers along with their stats all vying to review the product. You can check their blogs PageRank, DomainAuthority before you select them to receive the product. Since multiple bloggers will apply for the product, you'll get multiple links from credible sources at the same time.

98. Did Your Email Get Opened?

When you start contacting tens of people every day, for linkbuilding or PR or whatever, you need to be in the know on whether they opened your email or not. That way, you can see if your emails are working or are just getting sent into their Spam/Junk inbox. You need the power to know that, since you're sending emails at such a large scale. That's why you should use BananaTag (www.bananatag.com) , which is an email tracking system. It works for Gmail and Outlook, and is free for up to five emails a day that you want to track.

It also gives you the option to send emails at specific times automatically. If you write five emails in one go, and want them to be sent on a Tuesday in the afternoon (most likely time to be opened), you can schedule that with BananaTag.

99. Build Relationships With Your Niche's Key Influencers

Building and maintaining a great relationship with some of your niche's key influencers will give you a lot of leverage in the years to come. The best way to get key influencers to know you is to use social media and become an active commenter on their blog.

When they post a personal status update, comment back. For example, if they achieved something, congratulate them.

On Twitter, retweet some of their tweets and then, start commenting on their tweets too. Be smart in your comments and always add a personalized touch. You could also tweet something like, "My favourite blog is @SomeBlog'sHandle. I love the fact that it answers every question I have about #random_hashtag.". Make sure to use their Twitter handle (username, with the @ in front) so that they get notified of their mentioning.

Comment on a few of their blog posts and give praise. This lets them know that you are a great fan of theirs and enjoy reading about that niche. It shows that you are a real person with an interest (and a great website, may I add!), not just an anonymous 'botface'.

100. How To Find Influencers on Twitter
With a new tool called SocialBro (www.socialbro.com), you can identify influencers on Twitter who are following you. Because they are following you, you might find it easier to contact them since they have made some sort connection with you before.

Sign up for a free account and you can start finding people to both share your content and link to it, quickly and easily. This tool can also filter the number of followers people have, how long they were on the site, how influential they are and so on. This allows you to narrow down your list in a short time.

101. See Who Mentions You On Social Media, And Ask Them For A Link
If you or your brand gets mentioned on social media, you should approach that person and see if they've got a website. If they do, you can ask them for a link. But, make sure that their website is in the same niche as yours!

102. Monitor Your Social Media Mentioning At A Larger Scale
If your brand gets mentioned more than a few times a day on social media, you'll need to automate the process of recording the people who mentioned your brand.

For larger scale social media monitoring, you will need to use a free tool called RowFeeder (www.rowfeeder.com). This tracks and records all the social media posts from Twitter and Facebook which contains your name or username and your website's hashtag or keyword. All the reporting is done in Excel, allowing you to track who's talking about you, and what they're saying. This list in Excel will continue to grow, meaning that you will get a list of potential people for outreach. If they mentioned you on social media, they're more than likely going to mention you on their website!

103. Mention Key Influencers In A Blog Post, And They'll Link Back
If you mention some of the main key influencers in your niche, in a blog post, they are more than likely going to share your post on social media because of their ego. It's a quick way to get a lot of social media traffic to your site and in turn, a lot more exposure. Since these influencers have tens of thousands of social media followers, a lot of people will get to know your site and may even link back to it, if they like what the website or service has to offer.

To avail of this strategy, make a post called something like these; "5 [Your Niche] Rising Stars You Need To Watch" , "7 [Your Niche] Experts That Provide The Best Advice Every Time", "4 [Your Niche] [People] We Can't Help But Love" or "Top 5 [People] Making A Massive Stamp On [Niche]. Write about their life story, their achievements and their path to success.

Send them a quick email saying that you featured them in an article you've just written and give the link to the article.

Chances are, they'll probably share it on social media to the thousands and link to it on their own website.

Viral Linkbuilding With Infographics

104. Get Linkbuilding (and Go Viral) With Infographics
Infographics combine the best of graphic design and information, ie: displaying information such as statistics and facts using graphics, images and colour making it easy to digest. Infographics are all in the range right now, you see them on Pinterest, on Facebook and all over the most popular blogs and news websites. Infographics are quick to create, when you consider the amount of traffic that will be arriving to your website after seeing the infographic.

No one really knows why infographics rose to fame in the way that they did. But all I know is that if you want to have a chance of competing online, you need to start producing viral-worthy infographics.

And it's a lot easier than you think. Learn how to make infographics in Chapter 10.

105. Refresh An Old Infographic
For example, let's say I have found an infographic about social media statistics for 2013. That year is in the past, it's boring and it's no longer relevant to us. An infographic on 2015 or 2016 is so much more appealing than one made a couple of years ago. Sound appetizing? Here's how to give it a go.

Firstly, search for some real old infographics using the following search strings:
"infographic" [your niche]
"infographic" [your niche] 2013
"infographic" [your niche] stats 2013
"infographic" [your niche] facts 2013

You should find at least five minimum, all the way up to twenty. Check out some of the infographics which you suspect may be out of date. The best way to find out is to see if they have a year in their title, description or in the search result itself.

1) Select an infographic you think is ideal and copy its URL. This link will be used later on.

Since these are in your niche, I'm sure you can create an infographic of your own that covers the same topics as the out of date ones you saw in Google's results. You don't need to hire anyone, it is very easy to do it yourself.

2) Make the infographic by following the tips in Chapter 10, or else – hire a freelance designer on Elance to do it for you. Keep the statistics fresh and up to date. Make the design more appealing than the old infographic.

3) Get the URL of the infographic that is out of date.
Next, you will need to find out who exactly is linking to this particular infographic. Tapping into their backlinks is easy. Head over to www.ahrefs.com and create a free account by subscribing to their website. This web tool allows you to see how many backlinks a URL has – and where those backlinks are.

4) Input the link of the infographic you would like to check and the tool will track down how many backlinks that link has. Click on "Outgoing Links" in the horizontal bar and then "Links" which is in the dropdown menu. You will then be given a list of all the websites that link to that specific page.
Visit these linking pages and contact them saying that the infographic they were linking to is out of date and that you have a recent infographic with fresh and up to date facts and statistics.

106. Send This Template To The Blogger To Replace The Old Infographic Link
Here is a template you can use:
Hi [Blogger/Website Owner's Name],
I recently came across your page on [whatever category]. Here is the URL, [URL of page]. Great stuff! I just want to let you know that there is a link to an infographic by [Company/Website]. Here is the URL: [link]
As you can see, this infographic is out of date and provides little value to your readers. I have produced a new and up to date infographic which provides the same purpose as the one you are currently linking to. If you are willing to check it out, here it is: [your infographic URL].
As suiting the needs of the reader, I think that an up to date infographic will keep readers coming back to your website! Well done on that article, by the way and keep up the great work!

Thanks a whole lot!
[Your Name]

With a pitch like this, I think you can garner some pretty high PR backlinks from one image. Again, it takes time, work and a whole heap of effort but a template like the above takes a minute to paste in and send.

107. Infographic Guest Posting

Bloggers love free stuff and anything they can post onto their website without any work is golden. That's why you can write to bloggers telling them that you've created an infographic and that they can post it on their site free of charge.

This method is the same as guest posting only that instead of submitting an article to a blog, you submit an infographic instead. Create your infographic (or use the one you may have created from the last section) and make a list of all the blogs or websites that are similar to your website niche. Next, contact them with the following template which should give a pretty impressive response!

Hi [Blog Owner],
I recently came across your website on [topic]. What a fantastic place for [website's target audience]! I am the website owner of [Your URL] and I recently created an infographic about [topic]. I usually charge $[Price] for this infographic but I would love to give it to you for free since I am such a fan of your website! All I ask is that you provide a link to my website (where the infographic was first published) at the bottom of the infographic.
Oh, I nearly forgot! I will also write a unique and original introduction for the infographic too.
Let me know if you are interested.
Thanks a bunch!
[Your Name]

Try this out with a few websites and you should get some positive responses. You don't really charge anything for the infographic, but when they see that there is a price tag associated with it, that means value.

108. Make Sure You Have An Original Introduction To Your Infographic

Make sure that the introduction to each infographic is original and not used on the other websites you've submitted your infographic to. Always check that it is not published on other websites because Google will find out that you are not doing original backlinking and you will get caught out!

109. Submit To Infographic Submission Sites

As well as publishing on other websites, you can also submit your infographics to hundreds of infographic submission sites. Many of these sites have a high PageRank (we're talking 5, 6 and 7) so getting links on these is super beneficial. They also promote your infographic to their readers and email subscribers, so that will result in a lot of promotion to your brand!

Look for infographic submission sites with the following search strings:
"submit your infographic"
"infographic submissions"

110. Submit Your Infographic To Visual.ly (PageRank 8)

If you sign up for an account, you can submit an infographic to the site. If it is very appealing and informative, your infographic could be promoted on the homepage. I've seen infographics on visual.ly that got 30,000 views and higher. Since you are allowed a link back to your site, imagine all THAT traffic clicking in! From a Google-minded, backlinking perspective…you should get a hefty amount of link juice from that page too.

111. More Infographic Sites Include…

Other infographic submission sites include:
www.infographick.com – Free – PR 1
www.nfogfx.com – Free – PR 2
www.submitinfographics.com – Free – DA 53
www.infographicsite.com – Free – DA 29
www.coolinfographics.com – Free – DA 68
www.infographicpost.com – Free – DA 31

112. Create HTML Snippets Of Your Infographics
Make it easy for people to embed your infographic on their blogs. With a simple HTML snippet, bloggers can simply paste the code into their website and have another great infographic ready to publish! To generate a HTML snippet for your infographic, simply use the generator at SiegeMedia. (http://www.siegemedia.com/embed-code-generator)

Linkbuilding With Content

113. Make A Web App
If you have or develop a nifty online tool that'll solve a common problem internet users face, you've just got yourself a winner both for linkbuilding and exposure. You'll also develop a lot of brand awareness as a result. Tools such as calculators and converters but with an extra twist can really kick off online and spark a lot of media attention. For example, I've seen a web app which converted the number of alcohol units into food. For two units, it would be five burgers or one unit, it would be three donuts. It became very popular on social media and even got a mention from some major news websites and tech blogs!

Another advantage of web apps is that people will constantly link to it. For example, I just mentioned an infographic HTML snippet generator in the tip above. It's simple but effective and results in a lot of direct traffic to the site.

114. Make It Super Easy To Link To You
If your audience is less tech savvy, they mightn't know how to link to your content or embed anchor text on their blog. You can make it super easy for them to link to your page by generating a HTML snippet.

This is completely dependent on your niche though. If you're in a less tech savvy niche such as construction, pet grooming or gardening, your audience might want to copy the HTML snippet rather than link to your page with anchor text also.

Even for your readers who are complete tech geeks, a HTML snippet would speed up things for them too.

115. Rewriting An Out of Date Article

You don't need to use infographics for the "out of date" method. You need to find out of date articles in your niche. Try searching the following strings in Google:

[your niche] 2013
[your niche] 2012

Alternatively, try searching for old articles by websites such as Buzzfeed or Mashable.

These websites write articles on trending content and their information goes out of date very quickly. Today's viral article is next week's piece of internet history. You can take advantage of this. Try searching the following search strings into Google.

[your niche] Buzzfeed 2013
[your niche] Mashable 2012

The good thing is that these websites' articles get a TON of backlinks because they go viral every time. That means more backlinks for you to utilize, and more quality places to change the backlink to *your* content.

You can write an article which has updated and fresh information that contains all the essential facts for your year. For example, let's say you saw an article about the latest statistics on gender equality in the workplace. But that was written in 2012 and times have changed since then.

You can then see who is linking to this article through www.ahrefs.com and contact them saying your article contains statistics for 2015 or 2016. Rinse and repeat as many times as you want, and collect your links!

116. SlideShare Links

This PR 8 website with over 140 million views is a fantastic place to add a backlink. This website allows you to upload PowerPoint presentations and gain readers for them. It's basically a user generated content website for slide decks. You could repackage one of your blog posts into a SlideShare deck and upload it.

The advantage of using SlideShare is that you can gain thousands of readers, all to one deck! The audience on SlideShare is huge and provided you create a good thumbnail and title, you could be on the road to viral. A well placed backlink will bring back hundreds to your site.

The only downside of placing backlinks is that they are "nofollow" meaning Google don't take any notice of them, and no PageRank will flow to your site. However, SlideShare is still perfect for bringing thousands of potential customers to your site, even if you get no PageRank flowing to your site.

117. Written A News Post? Submit It To Google News
News sites have received more than 1 billion clicks, thanks to being listed on Google News. Getting one of your articles listed on Google News is huge. It can drive thousands of visitors to your site each day, if not more.

However, getting listed is not for the faint hearted.

Unless you publish at least once a day, you have no chance of being listed. Since "news sites" publish more than a few times a day, it is already assumed that your blog is publishing content on a daily basis. Also, your blog posts have to be written more like news articles, which provide facts, the inverted pyramid and no opinion.

However, if you meet the criteria of publishing *news* articles more than once a day, you can be listed on Google News along with a few other criteria.

Build up a constant supply of news articles every day, and after a few months – it's time to submit your website to Google News! Submit it at http://bit.ly/1aqAde4

118. Scoop.it Links Are Golden
Scoop.it is a curated content website which allows you to paste your favorite links across the web into a "scrapbook"-like page. Similar to Pinterest (where you Pin images onto subject specific boards), it allows you to create a collage of links about specific topics, eg: internet security or Spanish cooking. You can use Scoop.it to not only create your own boards but to suggest your article links to owners of other Scoop.it pages.

The advantage of getting links on Scoop.it pages is that they have a **high PR** (3 and 4) and an extremely large audience. There are literally thousands of pages which have garnered more than 20,000 views. Even tapping into a little of that audience would result in hundreds of views and excellent good link juice!

Set up an account with Scoop.it and head over to the arrow on the dropdown menu. You will find tens of Scoop.it pages related to your niche. You can then hit the "Suggest" button on these pages to suggest your links.

You can also create your own boards too over time. Make sure that you provide variety and a good mix of all the tutorials, articles and content related to your niche. Include some of yours too, but keep it to a minimum. Only linking to helpful and five star content will establish trust with your audience on Scoop.it and will gain traction once people start enjoying the content you link to.

119. Create A Free Icon Set And Get Links From Design Blogs

Design blogs are always linking to pages that offer free giveaways such as icon sets, website backgrounds, buttons and public domain images. Go to Fiverr and ask a graphic designer to create about ten icons that are about your niche. For example, if you run a technology blog, you can create icons of laptops, mouse cursors, smartphones and so on. These icons need to be compiled into a "free giveaway" and then, you can contact design blogs about your free icon set.

120. Been Snapping? Compile Your Images Into A Giveaway

Take a scroll through your images either on your camera or mobile phone, and see if you have any *non-personal* images that could really brighten up a blog post or website. For example, if you have any city, nature, landscape, food, technology or clothes shots, those would be perfect to be packaged into an "image giveaway". Basically, you give away these images for free provided you get attribution back to them. This is super effective for two reasons:

1) If you contact design blogs, and let them know you have a free giveaway of images – they'll go pretty crazy over it and will link back to your giveaway page whilst also promoting it non-stop on social media. These design blogs have a lot of followers both on email lists and on social media. That means more traffic and more potential leads to your website.

2) The people that want to use your images will have to provide attribution back to your website, leading to more backlinks and more link juice pointing back to your website. Of course, if those bloggers are not linking back to your photo, you can use the Google Reverse Image search method to find those neglected images.

Get Links From Journalists and Famous Bloggers

121. Join Help A Reporter Out (HARO)
This is by far one of my favourite linkbuilding strategies because of the exposure your website can get and the quality of links in return (PR 5, 6, 7, you name it).

Help A Reporter Out (HARO) allows journalists, members of the media and online writers to search for people that can answer questions they have in relation to a subject they know little about. They simply post their query on the HARO website and this query gets sent to 85,000 "sources" (everyday people who may have a deep knowledge or experience of a particular subject) by email each day.

Major news channels such as CNN, Fox News and The Huffington Post use HARO every day and there is a good chance you will find something you can be featured on. Over 50 queries are sent as one big email and delivered to your inbox every day.
You can scroll through the queries and see which websites are querying. This allows you to check their PageRank (through www.prchecker.info) and see if it's worth making a pitch to them. Most websites have a high PageRank and this allows you to get an extremely **powerful** backlink. Plus, your website will be featured on a website with an audience of thousands or millions.

To sign up, go to www.helpareporter.com and sign up for a free account. You can then fill in details about your brand such as your website URL or the name of your business (optional). Tick the boxes for the categories of HARO you would like to receive. The General HARO sums up what can be found in all the various HARO categories but if you want to be niche specific, you can sign up for Tech, Business or Lifestyle.

122. Use The "HARO Contributor Hack"
The dream of many: Gaining backlinks or referrals from industry experts...what could be better? Just imagine 50 experts/famous people in your field all linking to your content/website. You'd be famous)!

But how do you get people to share and link to your content?

The best way to do this is to do what I call the "Contributor Hack". All you have to do is send a query on HARO asking experts what their #1 trick is for …. (you fill in the blank).

Mention that their pitch can be from 50 – 200 words and that they will receive a backlink to their website. Since the question is so straightforward and relatively simple, you will get tons of responses from experts in your niche all vying for a backlink on your website. You might even get some new ideas you haven't heard of before.
Once you collect your responses, you can compile all of these into an expert roundup with the title such as *"50 [Niche] Experts Give Their #1 [Whatever] Trick For Success"*. eg: "50 SEO Experts Give Their #1 Linkbuilding Strategy For Success"

When you publish your article, you can respond to all the pitches by saying that their contribution was included in the article and send them over the link.

Since each and every one of the contributors helped in some way, they want to make it a success. They want all their followers, friends and family to see their contribution. This means that they will share it on social media, generating hundreds of indirect backlinks and may link to it on their own articles.

The advantage is that you can multiply the effect by 50 and the more contributors you have, the merrier. This little hack should really bring a huge amount of exposure to your website and leave 50 people do all the backlinking and promotion for you (with virtually no cost required).

Doing even two to three of these a year can mega boost your backlinks and bring back a TON of exposure to your site.

123. Tips For Making A HARO Pitch
I've used HARO many times, receiving hundreds of pitches when you count them all up. I've went through enough pitches for a lifetime, but certain pitches got onto the accepted list whilst a lot of them were thrown in the thrash. Here are the things you should keep in mind when pitching a journalist.

- **Be Personalized** – Use flattery. Say that you've read their articles before. Do whatever you can to sweeten those 'dead serious' writers up a little.
- **Don't Get Too Pushy** – Do not start rambling on about your website or company and the great things it does in the middle of your pitch. You can add that at the end of the pitch, where the journalist can go for more information on your website/company if they need it. Also, don't list out requirements for the journalist to use your pitch. I received something like this at the end of a pitch before, "If you want to use my pitch, please include my name, what I do, my company, my website and a link to my website too (for SEO purposes)."
- **Open and Close The Pitch** – Open the pitch by introducing who you are and why you would like to be a part of their article. Close the pitch by wishing them good luck with their article, and say thanks for them giving you the opportunity. It's simple but can really make your pitch stand out from the crowd.
- **Use Grammar and Correct Spelling** – Poor grammar and wrong spelling kills any chance you might have straight away. Type your pitch into a word processor and get it spell checked before you send it.

124. Contact A Local Journalist

Yes, journalists may have extremely busy lives and the chances a journalist will cover your story is slim – but do it right and you have a solid chance. I find that the best journalists to contact are the local journalists that write for your local newspaper (which is also online). Since there's less competition in your local area than in a national newspaper, you have a fairly good chance of getting a story done.

Also, since your local, you can also meet them in person for an interview which is always another incentive for journalists to write about your story.

If your company just launched, achieved an award or got a certain amount of sales – a journalist can easily turn this into an interesting story.

However, you need an interesting twist to make it a newsworthy story. It might be the fact that you're the only company in the country that sells that product or that you have the most customers in the region, within that niche.

125. Find Journalists With "Muck Rack"

Muck Rack (www.muckrack.com) allows you to find journalists related to your niche. By simply searching for your niche, you can find journalists which cover that topic. The free account gives you very limited access to search results, and you can only get a handful of journalists with each search. However, by purchasing a paid account (in the region of about $200 monthly), you can get full access to most of their features.

I have found this to be useful when trying to get "interesting" start up websites off the ground, and to get extremely high PR links back to a website. However, I wouldn't recommend using Mud Rack if you don't have a newsworthy story to share with them. Journalists are very choosey on what stories they want to cover, so the decision of contacting them is completely up to you.

126. Find British Journalists You Can Contact

If you're finding it difficult to locate niche specific journalists, you can find them all at www.journalisted.com. This site only covers journalists in the UK, and media outlets such as the Guardian and the BBC. There are over 30,000 British journalists at this site, so you are sure to find the perfect journalist to cover your story.

127. Sign Up To ProfNet, For More Media Opportunities

This is very similar to HARO, where you can sign up as an expert and receive queries from journalists or bloggers who want information or tips on a certain topic. Sign up to this, and you'll get queries to your inbox every day that are all related to your niche. You can sign up to both HARO and this, if you want to amplify your chances of receiving the perfect query.

It's completely free, and you can sign up as an expert at www.prnewswire.com/profnet

128. Personalize Your Email

Get them seriously thinking about covering you. The only way to do that is to personalize your email. Ask them a question about their latest project or event, eg: how their latest journalists' conference in Denver went. Give them compliments such as how much you enjoyed reading their feature about whatever.

*"The world revolves around me. Me, me, me. My favorite person: Me. I don't want email from you. I don't want junk mail from you. I want **me-mail**."*
— Seth Godin

You'll be surprised at how a little flattery can work.

When I asked SEO experts to send contributions, I got a lot which said "Hi there" or even worse, "Hi Sir". Ahem. #Facepalm
These emails were all about them, about their company, about their achievements and so on. It looked like their latest PR stunt. They were riding the gravy train, wanting to get a feature in a book.
Compare these with marketers who said "Hi Silvia", "Wow, I like the sound of your book!" and "I'm looking forward to reading your book, good luck with it!".

These contributions were featured (well, obviously the good ones were featured, I didn't pick them based on personalization, but as you can see – it still buttered me up), and now you can see why a little personalization will always guarantee success.
No matter what you do, always add some personalization. You'll be surprised at the results.

129. Common Outreach Email Mistakes
Here are a few things to never do when you're sending outreach emails to get links, guest posts or just for some plain simple promotion.

- **Being Blunt Hurts** – Don't make plans such as "I want to write a guest post for you. Please send me your response in 24 hours" or "I want two links to my blog in the guest post." Let them accept you first, and then you can start bargaining.
- **Super Long Email Signatures** – Avoid attaching a super long, ugly mess of an email signature including practically every little thing you've done in your life and every social media site you've ever joined. All you need is your name, company, personal website and a few social media channels. No more.
- **Sending Late In The Week** – Avoid sending your email on a Friday evening, or even on a Thursday. Chances are, it'll get drowned in an unfaltering mass of weekend email. Also, avoid sending emails on a Monday too. They'll be working on getting through all that weekend email, and your email could get ignored.
- **Blathering On About Your Company** – The email isn't a press release, always keep that in mind. Mention your company's/website's slogan or tell them what it does in a sentence.

130. Don't Email Multiple Journalists At Once
If you're trying to contact more than one journalist at a time just to "quicken things up", you're only wasting your time. It'll hit the trash pile quicker than you think. Always send a separate email to each journalist.

131. Give Journalists Everything They Need (Photos, Facts, Figures and a Press Release)
Don't give them a couple of sentences about what your story is about. Instead, give them photos, facts, statistics and even a press release if you have one. Journalists lead busy lives and the easier it is to write a story without contacting you for further information, the more you increase your chance of getting written about.

Getting Links For Stolen Content

132. Build Links Through Getting Your Content Scraped/Copied
Your content is bound to be copied at some stage, and for some webmasters – they find that their content has been copied hundreds or even thousands of times.

Even if you get the content taken down, there will always be another site that'll resurrect the copied content once more. A common problem for many, but get creative and you'll see that getting content copied can become a linkbuilding strategy.

In your content, add links to other blog posts you've written and add a note at the end of your article, as described below.

133. Add A Note At The End Of Your Article
Include a note like this at the end of your article:
"This article was written by Susan Wells on BlogName.com, on the 17th December 2015."
Add a link to the note by hyperlinking one of the words, back to the original article. That way, if your content gets copied or scraped, the note with the link will get copied too.

134. Image Attribution Links
After a couple of months, your site should start receiving daily traffic. This means that more and more people will be viewing it and checking out your content and images. If you have some steal-worthy images, that will lead to jealous bloggers and they may use your image on their blogs without any attribution. You have two options; leave them alone or get a link back to your site as attribution.

The best way to find out if other people have been stealing your images is to use Google Images reverse search feature. You can upload your images that you want to check and search for them. Google will then show you all the places this image is used online.

If any blogs or websites show up that aren't yours, your image has been stolen. However, this can be easily attended to. Since you caught out the person who did it (and using others' images is an offence), they have no option but to do as you say. Otherwise, you could report them for copyright infringement.
The following image will explain exactly how to use Google's Reverse Image Search to find stolen images. Professionals and stock image companies use this method all the time to find images that weren't attributed or paid for.

If you have found any images that aren't attributed or correctly following your license terms, it's time to make justice done (and get a backlink)!

Contact the webmaster with the following template:
Dear [Name],
I recently came across your content, [URL].
Great stuff! However, I noticed that the [number, eg: third] image you used of the [object] is my own work and has been used without attribution. Could you please link back to my website as attribution for the image? You can either link the image to my website or provide the link at the end of your article in the image credits section. Otherwise, I will have to take further action.
Thank you,
[Your Name]

This email will scare the webmaster severely. Further action could mean losing an AdSense account, losing their indexing on Google, losing their website hosting or just the complete shutting down of their website. The response rate for getting that backlink is extremely high since they want to avoid any trouble.

Google Reverse Image Search

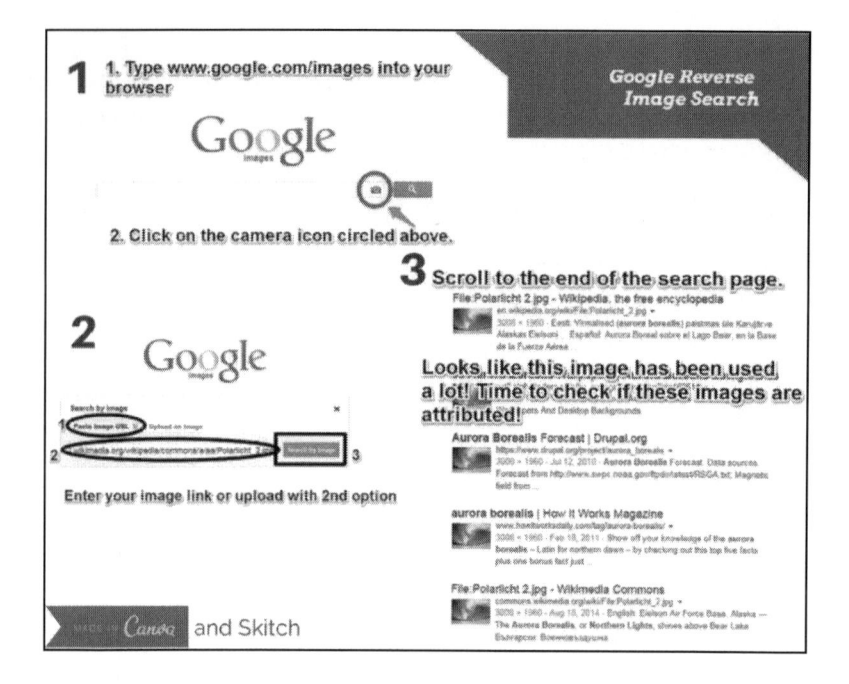

1. Type www.google.com/images into your browser
2. Click on the camera icon circled above.
3. Scroll to the end of the search page.

Enter your image link or upload with 2nd option

Looks like this image has been used a lot! Time to check if these images are attributed!

Made in Canva and Skitch

135. Send A Follow Up Email If You Don't Hear Anything Back
Sometimes, the person you're trying to reach made a simple mistake by forgetting to reply to your email, or fix the broken link or give attribution to your images. If you don't hear back from them after two weeks, it's time to follow up. You can add a reminder to your email

Or, you can use Boomerang Email (www.boomerangemail.com) which is a free email app that sends a follow up to that person, if they don't reply back within a certain time period. It also has a built-in function to give you reminders, such as if you need to contact someone later on or get a follow up. If outreach is a hefty part of your day, you will need this app for sure!

Broken Linkbuilding and Dead Content Linkbuilding

136. Broken Link Building
This tactic involves finding blogs that have broken links (links that point to pages that no longer exist, or content that was taken down) and then asking the webmaster if you can replace the broken link with your content. Follow these steps to find broken links on blogs in your niche:

1) Get a list of blogs in your niche. About five is plenty.
2) Input the links of these blogs into Buzzstream's list builder. This takes the links found on their blogroll and inserts them back into the list.
3) Download the results as a CSV and open it up in Excel. Copy and paste the links into the tool (which takes a max of 50 links) at www.seoautomatic.com/unique. This will check if any of the websites in the list show up as a 404 (no longer available). Make sure you the links include the HTTP header, ie: http://www.seoautomatic.com and not www.seoautomatic.com.
4) Copy the URLs of the websites which are no longer on the web, and enter them into www.ahrefs.com. This tool will show you which blogs and websites are linking to the website (which is a broken link for them).
5) Go to these websites and contact them with this template:

Hi [Name of Webmaster],
I'm a huge fan of your website/blog! I have noticed that you are linking to the website, www.disappeared-website.com and it is a broken link.
Since that website is no longer available, I was wondering if you wanted to link to this website [URL of your website] instead which focuses on [state aim of your website].
Thanks so much!
Kind Regards,
[Your Name]

137. Dead Content Broken Linkbuilding

That's quite a mouthful, isn't it? In reality, it's actually a simple strategy that you can use to build links.

1) Get the list of the 404 websites which are no longer available. Check the content on their blogs and make a list of their blog posts.
2) Plug these links into www.ahrefs.com and see which pages are linking to their content.
3) Take a visit to these websites and contact them with this template:

Hi [Name of Webmaster],
You've got some super helpful posts on your blog, and I'm an avid reader of them. I have noticed that you are linking to this piece of content which is a 404: www.disppeared.com/zero-nada and it is a broken link.

Since that page is no longer available, I was wondering if you wanted to link to my piece of content instead which is very similar to the old one. Let me know what you think.

Thanks so much!
Kind Regards,
[Your Name]

138. Find A Resource Page and Look For Broken Links
Get a resource page in your niche by entering the following search strings into Google:
"[your niche] + resources"
"[your niche] + best blog posts"
Download the "Check My Links" browser extension for Chrome and check the page for any broken links. Since it's a resource page and has tens of links, at least one or two of them should point to a no longer existing page.

139. Decide Which Websites To Get Broken Links From
When you notice that a website is linking to a 404 page that's gone off the web, you need to decide whether contacting that website is worth your time. Check for the following when you are deciding to get a broken link from that website:

- **More Than Twenty Links?** – Since the PageRank flows to all the links, you will get little PageRank (or link juice, as the experts like to call it) or barely any at all.
- **Spam Links** – If they are linking to spam sites such as "payday loan" sites, you don't exactly want your link beside theirs. It looks very dodgy and could get you penalized by Google.
- **Poor Quality Content** – If the content isn't of a high quality, you risk getting a low quality, spam link back to your site. Only get backlinks from websites that have high quality content which get a high PageRank as a result (from all the pages linking to them).
- **A Poor Quality Website Overall** – Use your own judgement on this. If the website has little or no authority in your niche, there's not much point in getting a backlink from them.

140. Don't Use Full URLs In Your Emails

If you have an extra-long link to a page of yours or theirs, you'd be better off hyperlinking a word instead. Super long links could trigger the spam filters of their email.

141. Give Them A Phone Call

I've tried this a few times, and it works. A full conversation converts so much better than an email. It's quick, it's instant and it'll hopefully help develop a relationship with that webmaster who might link to your website in future content of theirs or share your blog posts on Twitter.

142. Found An Old Website? Send This Template Instead

When on the hunt for links and fixing broken links, send the following email to websites that look like they were last updated in the 90s. Since the owner probably isn't maintaining the website anymore, you need to write a very quick and short email just to see if they are still maintaining the website.

Hi there,
Are you still updating your website, [Website URL]? I found a broken link that I'd like to point out to you.
Thanks,
[Your Name]

143. Get Wikipedia Backlinks

Wikipedia offer you the chance to add references at the end of their articles, allowing you the chance to submit your link.

The links in the References box are "nofollow" (no PageRank will flow to your site), but you can get a huge amount of referral traffic from their articles, since millions of people land on Wikipedia every day. Also, when citing their sources, people will link to your page. That's two major benefits, and you know what's even better? It isn't too difficult to get a backlink from Wikipedia. Here's a step by step guide:

1. Sign up for a free account at www.wikipedia.org
2. Build up some history, showing you're a responsible person by editing a few articles and fixing some broken links by linking to other people's content.

3. Go to www.wikigrabber.com and search for your niche. This tool basically tells you which pages need citation or have "dead links" (Wikipedia's definition of a link that is no longer active).
4. Submit your link instead of the dead link

Make sure that your content looks authoritative by making it lengthy, full of images and include backed-up statistics. This will greatly improve your chance of getting your link included.

144. Recreate The Page Again, For More Wikipedia Backlinks

If you've done the work, you'll find that it shouldn't be too difficult to get your link accepted. However, if you've failed – don't feel too bad. Use this method instead.

Use www.wikigrabber.com to find Wikipedia pages which have dead links, in your niche.
Or else, type this query into Google, *"site:wikipedia.org [niche] dead link"*
Once you've landed on the page with the dead link, use CTRL+F to find the dead link. No one deserves to scroll through those links.

Copy the URL of the dead link and enter it into the Wayback Machine, which shows you what the page looked like before it disappeared (www.archive.org/web).

Get the main "essence" of the article, and try to recreate it on your own website. ***Don't copy it***, but keep it similar enough, including the same statistics as the old article.

Submit your link to Wikipedia and watch it get accepted!

145. Get Even More Backlinks For Your Wikipedia Article

Once you have the backlink on Wikipedia, to replace the dead link, you can find out who else is linking to that page and reach out to them. The majority of Wikipedia references have tons of backlinks, so you'll have more than 50 backlinks all pointing to the dead link! That means, even more high quality links to your page.

Input the dead link into www.ahrefs.com and see who is linking to it. Reach out to them and let them know that they are linking to a no longer existing page.

Helping Another Webmaster Out, In Exchange For Links

146. Help Webmasters With Hacked Sites, And They'll Reward You
Hundreds of sites get hacked every day. Hacking a site usually involves adding spam pages to an established website. These spam pages usually are about "banned" topics. You'll find a lot of hacked websites sporting nasty words such as "payday loans" or other malicious words in the page's content, without even realizing it.

Getting these spam pages added to your website will become quite an ordeal because Google could deindex you permanently from their index or lower your ranking in the SERPS severely.

That's why, if you can spot that a website is hacked, they'll reward you wholeheartedly (a link to your website, or even two). To find hacked websites, simply enter this search string into Google. Type your niche in the string below to replace 'gardening'.

"[Inurl: gardening+payday loans]"

Once you have found it, contact the webmaster saying you found some hacked pages on their website and that they need to remove them fast. Because you've helped them tremendously, they'll reward you very generously for it.

147. Update An Old Piece of Content and Get A Link In Return
Help a fellow blogger out by updating any old pieces of content that they have. You have a good chance of getting a link in return for helping them.

Search for old blog posts by pasting the website URL into www.ahrefs.com and look at their top pages. Chances are, some of the pages have been written more than three years ago.

Send them an email asking if you can update their content. Tell them who you are and your experience in the area.

When updating the content, refresh statistics and provide research that was done in the last year. Take out terms that are no longer used anymore (blogosphere, yeah?) or introduce new ideas and technologies that have become popular today.

148. Update Their Contests
A lot of websites have started contests or handed out awards, a couple of years ago but never got round to doing it this year. You can get a very valuable backlink by offering to organize a new contest for them this year, for free.

Do a couple of searches like these:
"2010 blogger awards"
"2006 best photo awards"
"2013 upcycling contest"
Locate the websites that have these contests. Do an internal search on their website to see if they had a contest this year or last year. If they didn't, it means they never got round to doing another contest for this year. You can step in and help them organize a new contest, and get the whole show back on the road again.

It doesn't take that much time or effort. All you need to do is open it on social media, accept submissions, pick out the best and give them awards. The website hosting the contest will have all the resources you need such as prizes, badges and so on.

149. Transcribe A Video
Video creation is a very popular content strategy at the moment, with lots of bloggers taking part in the action. However, many bloggers either don't bother putting a video transcript along with the video or simply don't have the time to do so. Writing a video transcript can take quite a long time! Since Google prefers to have a lot of text on the page, rather than a sole (and very lonely) video – getting a video transcript on the page can really boost quality metrics and gain trust. It's also super handy for people with slow internet speed. Instead of trying to load up your video, they can read the video transcript instead.

Search for some videos related to your niche using these strings:
"[your niche] video"
"[hobby in your niche] video"

Once you have found some videos, check to see if they have transcripts underneath them. If they don't, send the following template to the blogger in charge of that video or page:

Hi [Blogger's Name],
Firstly, I'd like to say that I'm a huge fan of your blog! As a fellow [niche person, eg: scientist], I think that your blog is an essential for gaining more valuable tips on [niche]. I was recently watching your <u>video</u> [link to video page] on [whatever the video is about] and I really enjoyed it! I found your point on [something] very useful!

Since the video provides so much value to your viewers, I'd love to transcribe the video for you completely free of charge.

Let me know what you think,
[Your Name]

150. Translate Content
If you're lucky enough to know a second language, you can use your language skills and translate an English page into the language of your choice.

There's always someone who'll take a quick shortcut, and this tactic is no exception. Whatever you do, don't try to translate the page using Google Translate. That tool still has major grammar issues and it'll probably result in a lot of unhappy readers. So, unless you're a native speaker of the language and know it fluently – don't go near this strategy.

Contact a webmaster saying that you'd like to translate one of their pages and see what they say. If you comment regularly on their blog and follow them on Twitter, you might just have a better chance. Once you've translated the page, provide a link back to your website or ask them to link to your website for you by adding a note at the end of the transcription saying *"This video was transcribed by [Your Name], blogger at [Your Website Domain]."*

Other Magical Linkbuilding Techniques

151. Create A "Subscribe To Get Email" Landing Page And Link To It In Your Guest Posts –
If you want to build your email list or your newsletter list, the best way to do it is by following the steps below.

Create a landing page for your email. Offer something in return for their email address such as an eBook, short course or a "step by step blueprint". In one sentence, mention why they should join your email list. It could be "insanely actionable tips straight to your inbox" or "Join 35,000 smart folks who get our best strategies every week". Look at the way well-known companies phrase this, and you should get some interesting ideas.

Make sure to mention that their email address is safe, secure and will not be sold to third part companies. You know, the usual.

When you write a guest post, link to your landing page in the "About The Author" section of the guest post and have something like, "Rachel also writes tutorials on her design blog. Join Rachel's email list to get insanely useful design tips and templates to your inbox. Plus, you'll be sent the "Step By Step Blueprint To Designing Beautiful Websites" when you sign up."

152. Create Coupon Codes/Special Offers For Other Blogs' Readers

You should create a secret page on your website that has a special offer for a product/service that you provide. If you don't sell products or services, you can create an ebook about your niche instead. If you write blog posts, you can just repackage all of them into an ebook. Then, when you are guest blogging on various blogs – add a link to your coupon code/discount/product either in the middle of the post or at the end. It can be a great incentive for readers to join your email list or become a customer of your website.

153. Pay Guest Bloggers To Write On Your Site

This tip can be a little controversial to some but when used, even once or twice a year, it can produce fantastic results. It involves paying a well-known blogger to write a guest post on your site. Once the guest post is published, they will share it on their well-stocked social media channels (with potentially hundreds of thousands of followers), leading to hundreds or thousands of people arriving at your site, with a lot of them becoming customers.

Bloggers love getting paid to write, so it'll be very easy to get a blogger to write a guest post for you. They'll also link to your post in their future blog posts, and will share on social media – resulting in even more backlinks (if others pick up on your content, and link to it in their content).

Contact a well-known blogger or influencer in your field to write a guest post on your site (with more than five thousand followers on Twitter) and tell them that you will pay them to write a guest post on your site. Offer anything in the region of $50 to $200, depending on how many followers they have and other metrics. Say what you'd like them to write about. A general topic is fine, don't get too detailed.

Once they have it written, pay them (PayPal is usually the best option) and publish it! The writer will then share it on social media and you'll get a good influx of traffic to your site!

You don't need to do this more than twice a year, since it can be quite costly.

154. Sponsor An Event If You're A Local Business
If there are events or festivals or charity events being held in your local town or city, you can sponsor them and they are sure to give you a backlink on their website. It will give you not only a backlink but a lot of exposure in your local community that could lead to many more customers.

It is costly to sponsor even a small event so make sure to weigh up the potential benefit that it would have on your company. If you deal with mainly online sales from other countries or parts of the country, you will find it difficult to supplement your income from the local town too. But if your company deals with many local customers or clients, you should definitely take sponsorship into consideration.

155. Internal Links Work Wonders
You might find that upon entry to Buzzfeed, you start reading one article they've written but suddenly, another article title catches your eye in the "Popular On Buzfeed" section and you click on it, wanting to read more.

Apply the same technique as Buzzfeed, to your website and you'll draw more readers further into your site. Plus, the pages will give a lot of PageRank to each other too.

156. Link To Your Best Content On Your Homepage
Include a "Popular Posts" section which contains links to your best content. When you get a backlink to your homepage, all the juicy PageRank will flow to the other articles too.

157. Research Your Competitors With Ahrefs.com
Try out stealing your competitor's strategies and see where they have been linkbuilding. Since they are in the same niche as you, it's possible to see which websites gave them guest posts, where they submitted their infographics and so forth.

Get the link to your competitor's website and paste it into www.ahrefs.com. This handy tool shows you how many backlinks they have, what anchor text they are using, what pages have been linking to them and more. You'll need to sign up to a free account to use it more than once per day.

158. No Competition? Try Out Overseas Competitor Research

Some rare websites find that there are no websites or companies offering the same product/service as theirs or that there are no blogs writing on the same niche. This means that they find it difficult to do competitor research and find out where others have been linkbuilding.

You get more links back to your content, and you alert readers that the blog that they're reading are nothing more than content thieves.

All you have to do is search for your competition on a Google search engine from another country. Type the URL of the foreign Google search engine, and then follow it with "ncr" which stands for No Country Redirect, eg: www.google.es/ncr

159. Get Links From LinkProspector

It's often said that you shouldn't automate the process of link building and that software will never be able to change the fact that link automation equals web spam.

But LinkProspector is going to change that.

Developed by Citation Labs, this online tool allows you to find high quality links by searching for blogs that allow guest posts, influencers who will link to your content, bloggers that will repost your infographics, blogs that advertise giveaways for free and resource pages that will link to you.

Basically, it cuts out the tedious task of finding links manually, and gives you the opportunity of finding tons of high quality pages you can outreach. You still have to contact the webmaster manually, but it still cuts the work in half.

Obviously, the tool isn't completely perfect yet and you will still need to search for opportunities using all the tips in this chapter. But if you scan through the results, you'll find some very worthy opportunities.

It's free for one credit or one search, and after that, it costs $2.00 per search. This is great value considering each search will give you hundreds of link opportunities. Start now by signing up at www.linkprospector.citationlabs.com.

160. Google Alerts

Google Alerts is a neat tool that lets you know when certain "phrases" are mentioned on the web, such as new events or the mentioning of a company. Set up Google Alerts so that when your company (or your name) is mentioned on the web, you can ask the writer to provide a backlink to your site. Rather than just mentioning your company or website, they can also link back to it.

If you're lucky enough for your name to be featured in an article, you can also ask the writer to link back to either your personal site or company website.

161. Get Backlinking Opportunities From Flippa

Flippa (www.flippa.com) is a marketplace that allows you to buy and sell websites. A lot of the webmasters that are selling their websites, provide additional notes on their SEO efforts such as keywords and backlink sources. It's like getting an entire blueprint to their SEO strategies and techniques.

Go to Flippa and search for your niche. You'll find hundreds of sites which are being sold, along with their SEO strategies outlined. This means you can tap into their backlinking and see where they got their backlinks. If they're in your niche, and can get backlinks – so can you.

162. Crowdfunding Backlinks

Whilst you shouldn't be paying for links, some websites offer a link back to your website from their website if you donate a certain amount to their company or startup. However, you should make sure that the website linking back to your website is related to your niche. You don't want a fitness blog linking back to your website on cars...talk about dodgy!

Also, you will develop a new contact with a website owner or blogger who wants to work with you in the future, since you helped them fund their company even if it was a small amount.
You kill two birds with the one stone.
You get a link back to your website from a popular website (in the future, depending on whether they become successful) and you are helping to fund exciting new innovations, technologies and projects.

163. Watch Out For Anchor Text, Keep It Varied
When you link to your website, you need to hyperlink a word in the form of anchor text. For example, if you wanted to link back to a post you've written, you would hyperlink the word in the guest post (in bold here) - "Linkbuilding is an essential strategy that every webmaster should continue to use even post Panda. Whilst **guest posting** is a common linkbuilding practice, it should be noted that there are tens of other ways to get backlinks!." The word "guest posting" is known as anchor text.

If you are linking back to the same webpage more than a few times, make sure to vary the anchor text, ie: hyperlink different words each time. For example, if you linked to the same post three times, the following words would be excellent as anchor text, "guest posting", "how to guest post effectively" or "guest posting for beginners".

This is also very beneficial for the Hummingbird update which tries to actually understand the content from a more human perspective and not just as a robot. When it sees various differentiations of the anchor text, it is able to "Understand" the words a lot more and thus, place more relevance on the article.

164. Is Your Anchor Text Over Optimized?
Having too much over optimized (keyword stuffed) anchor text can signal real alarm bells for Google. For example, let's say you kept linking back to your tomato growing article with the text, "how to grow tomatoes". You might have a few other variations of anchor text for other links, but over half of the anchor text pointing back to your tomato growing article page has the same anchor text. That would be a purely black hat SEO technique and it will get you penalized severely.

That's why you should check your anchor text from time to time. The best way to do this is by using the tool at, www.removeem.com/ratios.php. Simply input the link and you will get a word cloud showing all the anchor text that points back to that page.

165. If Your Brand Name Is Over Optimized, That's Fine
When you're building links and creating anchor text, don't get too worried if you want to leave your brand name as the anchor text. Similarly, if you used the tool above that checks over optimization of anchor text, don't get too worried if your brand name is over optimized. You should only get worried if you are over optimized for *keywords*.

166. Black Hat Linkbuilding Should Be Avoided
Never, ever resort to black hat linkbuilding such as link automation software or buying tacky links from link farms. Doing this will close down your site sooner or later (in the next Penguin update, you will be crushed) because Google will keep fighting to kill these black hat websites.

167. Don't Get Lured Into Black Hat Traps
I often get emails from SEOs saying that they will link to my website ten times if I pay them $10 or whatever. These people usually own websites with PageRank of 0 or even N/A (Not Available). Getting links from them would be extremely harmful to any website.

Google is one intelligent monster that's going to find out. If it knows you're age, interests, health condition, nationality, hobbies, location, family and favourite websites – it's certainly going to know if you've been exchanging links for money. Backlinks should be built through trust and certainly not money.

So no matter what you come across on the web, never get lured into black hat traps. It's fatal for your website and could undo all the work you've ever done on it.

168. Get Alerted When Someone Links To Your Site

It's always a cause for celebration when you get a valuable backlink from another site. With Linkstant (www.linkstant.com), you can get updates almost instantly when your website gets a backlink. The notification can be sent through email or SMS, and will give you all the useful details such as URL, website name, anchor text and much more. After you've done your outreach, broken linkbuilding and whatnot, you can finally get notified on whether the work is getting you somewhere!

169. Check To See If A Website Got A Penalty

Sometimes, you will need to check if a website got a penalty from Panda or Penguin. If they did, it's clear that perhaps you shouldn't get a link from their site. If Google distrusts them, they could value your link as being poor or even worse, spam.

Whilst this isn't necessary for all websites you hope to get links from, you should use it for those websites that you aren't quite sure about. Note that traffic estimates are very vague, so don't take them very accurately. The traffic data is only there to give you a general indicator. (www.feinternational.com/website-penalty-indicator/)

CHAPTER 5
Thriving In A Post Panda and Penguin World

Google need to be able to read your site and index it without getting caught up. If your website is not optimized for crawlers (used by Google to scan your website), you will find that Google cannot index your content. If your website provides a poor user experience, Google may not rank you as high as you hope. All your SEO can go down the drain should your technical aspects let you down.

This chapter will help you get a handle of the technicalities you need to get indexed and ranking well. You'll also learn to make sure that Google can read, index and rank your site with ease.

170. User Experience Matters
Deliver an excellent user experience with; faster PageSpeed, easy navigation, static pages and great content.

171. Don't Do A Ton Of Backlinking All At Once
This is because it will result in an unnatural spike in backlinks, making it look like the backlinks are artificial. Keep your backlinking efforts at a very slow yet constant pace. Getting three powerful backlinks spread across a week is good practice, rather than the same all in one day.

172. Watch Your Keyword Density
is the amount of times a specific keyword is used within a page. It is used as a percentage, ie: the (number of times it appears over the total amount of words) x 100. The ideal keyword density for your chosen keyword should be about **1.5%-3%**. Never exceed more than 3%, because it is viewed as spam in Google's eyes. Don't even worry about keyword density because it is not a major ranking factor – just don't overdo any keywords.

173. Content Is King

An age-old cliché can be surprisingly correct. Great content is your key to Google domination, because many websites can't be bothered to do the work. 1500 words may sound like a curse plagued upon you but it's shorter than you think. As a beginning writer, it took me about five hours straight to get that nailed plus a few images. These days, I can type my way to 1500 in about two hours. Once you begin, it will get easier and easier. The time it takes you to write great content is less than the amount of backlinking you would have to do to match that.

174. Appeal To The Hummingbird

The Hummingbird update is all about understanding the searcher's query at a human level, and providing answers which solves their problem. You need to optimize not just for Panda/Penguin updates but also for Hummingbird.

Make your pages as fluent and natural as possible. Don't make it look like you're trying to make money, but rather that you want to offer the answer to the users search. This means epic content, LSI keywords (synonyms, words related to your targeted keyword) and a more conversational way of writing.

175. Delete Any Pre-Panda Pages You Have

Get rid of any poor quality pages you may have, ie: **thin, duplicate, short, unhelpful or spun pages.** Once these are gotten rid of, your website will receive a new burst of life.

176. Vary The Kinds Of Anchor Text You Use

Don't keep hyperlinking the same keywords every time because it looks very unnatural to see anchor text so similar. Instead, target different keywords in your anchor text. For example, if you linked back to your content on smoking salmon three times, the anchor text could be: "smoked salmon", "how to smoke salmon" and "salmon smoking". This diversity really looks impressive!

177. Is Your Content Authoritative?

According to the Google Webmaster Central blog, here are some questions you should be asking yourself when it comes to both your website and the content you create.

- Would you trust the information presented in this article?
- Is this article written by expert/enthusiast who knows the topic well, or is it more shallow in nature?
- Is the site a recognized authority on its topic?
- Would you recognize this site as an authoritative source when mentioned by name?
- Is this the sort of page you'd want to bookmark, share with a friend, or recommend?

The essential thing to take away from this tip is that you need to demonstrate authority on your niche. This means that you need to know the subject well, write about it in-depth and making it "bookmarkable" and shareable. Go the extra mile by adding statistics and even a few personal experiences.

178. Be A Grammar Geek, It Helps

The Panda updates are also stamping down on poor grammar, since it demonstrates a lack of authority on the subject and also weakens the user experience. Make sure to check your spelling and grammar throughout every page on your website, and in every blog post that you write.

Whilst there is no need to go too overboard on it, just keep in mind that Google favors sites with excellent writing that is thorough, has no obvious grammar or spelling mistakes and easy to both read and understand (this varies depending on the audience).

179. Read What Google Webmasters Have To Say About "Making A High Quality Website"

Google have a rather lengthy list of questions you can use to see if the content you are providing is Panda friendly and if it's considered high quality by Google. Read through this list and try to adhere to the guidelines.

- Would you trust the information presented in this article?
- Is this article written by an expert or enthusiast who knows the topic well, or is it more shallow in nature?
- Does the site have duplicate, overlapping, or redundant articles on the same or similar topics with slightly different keyword variations?

CHAPTER 5: THRIVING IN A POST PANDA AND PENGUIN WORLD

- Would you be comfortable giving your credit card information to this site?

- Does this article have spelling, stylistic, or factual errors?

- Are the topics driven by genuine interests of readers of the site, or does the site generate content by attempting to guess what might rank well in search engines?

- Does the article provide original content or information, original reporting, original research, or original analysis?

- Does the page provide substantial value when compared to other pages in search results?

- How much quality control is done on content?

- Does the article describe both sides of a story?

- Is the site a recognized authority on its topic?

- Is the content mass-produced by or outsourced to a large number of creators, or spread across a large network of sites, so that individual pages or sites don't get as much attention or care?

- Was the article edited well, or does it appear sloppy or hastily produced?

- For a health related query, would you trust information from this site?

- Would you recognize this site as an authoritative source when mentioned by name?

- Does this article provide a complete or comprehensive description of the topic?

- Does this article contain insightful analysis or interesting information that is beyond obvious?

- Is this the sort of page you'd want to bookmark, share with a friend, or recommend?

- Does this article have an excessive amount of ads that distract from or interfere with the main content?

- Would you expect to see this article in a printed magazine, encyclopedia or book?

- Are the articles short, unsubstantial, or otherwise lacking in helpful specifics?

- Are the pages produced with great care and attention to detail vs. less attention to detail?

- Would users complain when they see pages from this site?

from Google Webmaster Tools blog

180. Follow Google Webmasters on Social Media
Google have exceptional social media profiles (obviously) and almost every day, you'll get updates on the latest news, algorithms and also a wealth of SEO and web development tips.

181. Build Nofollow Links To Make Your Backlink Profile More Natural
If Google see that all of your links pass PageRank (dofollow links), they know that you've been building links for SEO purposes only and you didn't get them naturally.
By building a few nofollow links, it'll make your backlink profile look more natural and diverse. Some great places to get nofollow links are blog comments (no comment spam, though!), Wikipedia References links and Slideshare links.

182. Don't Trade Links With Other Bloggers
If I link to your blog, you have to link back to mine. This is known as trading links or reciprocal links. You'd think that this would positively impact on both your websites, but you'd be very wrong.

You've probably learned in math class that a positive number and a negative number cancel out each other, if they're the same, eg: -2 and +2 cancel out and equal zero.
Apply this theory to trading links and you'll see what you get. Getting a link, and giving one in return cancels out the two of them. This gives a very obvious indication that you've been exchanging links.

Google want links to show that you're website is worth watching (in a good way), not to give someone a favor.
A lot of experts still say that trading links is still an okay practice, but there's no point since the links will cancel each other out anyway.

183. Use Only Trustworthy Advertisers

If you give dodgy sites an advertising space on your website, these ads could be demolishing the trust that Google has with your website. Make sure to check the ads that are being featured on your website, and that they are credible. Don't sell ad space to any spam sites, or sites which lack Google's trust. Otherwise, you could be showing the wrong signals.

184. Keep Advertising Beneath The Fold

The term "above the fold" means it's the content that loads up on the page, without you having to scroll down. Basically, the first "screen" of content that appears on your computer. Try to keep your advertising underneath this first screenshot, in other words, you have to scroll down to start seeing ads.

The advantages of this is that Google gets the impression that you're not a spam site (which love plastering the top of their webpages with dodgy ads). Also, it'll get your page loading up faster.
If you rely heavily on advertising income, and cannot afford to get rid of ads that are above the fold, try to reduce the number that you have.

If your website has been penalized by Google in the past and you're trying to recover – it would be worth decreasing the number of ads that you have above the fold.

185. Check That Other Site's Aren't Copying or Spinning Your Content

The last thing you want is to get penalized by Google because other sites have spun your content...and you're the person getting the blame. I've learned it the hard way by not checking my content for duplicates. When I eventually did (after a nasty Google algorithm update), I discovered my content had been duplicated more than fifteen times on multiple sites.

Prevent this disaster by doing one of the following checks on your content. It's best to check all of your content including blog posts, static website pages and anything else.

186. Search A Snippet Of Your Content and Check For Duplicates

Pick a random snippet from your blog post (about one sentence in length) and enter it into Google. Basically, if another website has that exact snippet, you should be getting suspicious!

187. Check For Duplicates With Copyscape.com
Copy and paste your entire blog post into the text box on www.copyscape.com. This super handy tool will let you know if anyone has been duplicating your blog post.

188. Found Duplicates of Your Content? Contact The Webmaster
If in the very likely event, you find that your content has been duplicated on other websites, you need to take action by getting those duplicates taken down. The first step is to contact the webmaster who is in charge of editing the site and/or creating the content. Send them the following email:

Dear Sir/Madam,
I am the owner of the following website, www.yourwebsite.com *and I have written a blog post which can be found here* www.yourwebsite.com/your-content.
I have found that you have duplicated my content which can be found here: www.theirwebsite.com/duplicated-content.
Please remove this content from your website immediately.
Otherwise, I will have to file a complaint against your website.
Regards,
Your Name

189. No Contact Details? Get Their Contact Details Through WHOIS
Some websites are sneaky enough to have no contact details whatsoever, making it impossible to contact them. No worries though, you can get their exact contact details through www.whois.com. Search for their website domain on this site, and you should see that their contact details are right there.

However, some website owners keep their contact details confidential by getting their website domain signed up with private registration. This is not the easy route to being impossible to track down. It's still possible to get the duplicated content removed and this is through contacting their hosting service.

190. Get The Entire Website Removed By Contacting Their Hosting Service

You will find that most webmasters will take down the content immediately, since they don't want their entire website taken down by their hosting. However, there are still a lot of thieves out there who won't bat an eyelid to the email you just sent.

Instead, you need to hit them where it hurts most – getting their website taken down by their hosting service.

You can find out who is hosting the website by paying a visit to www.whoishostingthis.com. Input the URL of the website and you should see who is hosting the website. Get their contact details and send them an email like this:

Dear Sir/Madam,
I am the owner of the website, www.yourwebsite.com and I have written a blog post which can be found at: www.yourwebsite.com/your-content.
I would like to bring to your attention that the website which is being hosted by your service, www.awebsite.com has been duplicating my content. The duplicated content can be found here www.awebsite.com/duplicated-content.
I have sent them an email already to remove the content but they have not removed the content yet. I have no reason but to file a DMCA complaint if they do not take down the duplicated content.
Regards,
Your Name

191. Kick Out Pages With No Traffic

If you have a lot of stale pages that no one is bothering to read and pages that aren't getting any search traffic, it looks terrible in Google's eyes. It shows that your website is not authoritative on the subject and must not be relevant to search users. This means that these flat pages that get no traffic could be pulling your entire site down.

Either tweak the content on these pages to get social media traffic (more on this later on) or change the targeted keywords. If that doesn't work, just delete these pages from your website.
You'll even find an increase in traffic once you do this, because the higher quality websites won't be weighed down by the stale pages.

192. Imitate What You Like Most
Panda is all about epic content and it's the websites with the most epic content that always wins. Sometimes the best strategy for prospering during Panda is imitating what you like most, ie: what content do you like to read? Maybe it's innovative techniques, or posts with lots of juicy facts and statistics or posts with charts, diagrams and engaging visuals.
Most people like the exact same type of content that you do, so by tailoring your content and making it similar to the type of content you like – it can do the same to thousands of other people.

193. Get Rid of Outdated Pages
There's a huge difference between evergreen content and outdated content. Evergreen content is content that will remain relevant and up to date even five years from now, eg: gardening tips or DIY tutorials. Many websites still have articles from over ten years ago which are up to date even today. However, outdated content could be written only two years ago and be completely out of date today, eg: old news, old scientific findings or technology articles.
If you have any articles that are completely outdated and you cannot make any changes to refresh them and make them current, just get rid of them.

194. Were You Affected By Panda? Check With This Tool
I've found this tool to be very useful over the years, especially when Panda and Penguin updates are rolled out. It basically shows your web traffic for the last few months, and displays when specific algorithm updates rolled out. You can then see if you got a drop in traffic, or rarely – an increase in traffic. It partners with your Google Analytics data so you get the most accurate traffic data. Quite a handy tool! (www.barracuda-digital.co.uk/panguin-tool/)

195. How "Stormy" Were The Rankings This Week?
Get a weather forecast…for Google's rankings! This daily forecast displays if the rankings have been turbulent this week or if Google rolled out a new algorithm update. The hotter the temperature, the more "stormy" the rankings are. It's a little vague but still worth a look. Check it out at www.mozcast.com.

CHAPTER 6

Technical SEO

Google need to be able to read your site and index it without getting caught up. If your website is not optimized for crawlers (used by Google to scan your website), you will find that Google cannot index your content. If your website provides a poor user experience, Google may not rank you as high as you hope.

All your SEO can go down the drain should your technical aspects let you down.

This chapter will help you get a handle of the technicalities you need to get indexed and ranking well. You'll also learn to make sure that Google can read, index and rank your site with ease.

196. Make Sure You Join Google Webmaster Tools
For spotting technical errors and for getting a constant status update on how Google crawled your site, and any issues it found - sign up your website to Google Webmaster Tools. It gives you practically everything you need to make sure your website is working very well technically and that Google is indexing and crawling your website correctly.

197. Join Bing Webmaster Tools
Most webmasters focus on Google alone and don't really put as much effort into other search engines. However, depending on your demographics (an older audience), you may still need to use Bing. Also, Bing still gets a hefty amount of the world's daily searches by occupying 2.5% of the world's daily searches. It's still worth optimizing for regardless, and could still bring you hundreds of readers a day should you do it right.

198. Understand The Crawling and Indexing Process
When your website is live, Googlebots will head over to your website's pages. They will gather information such as the keywords used, length of content and linking patterns. They basically inspect each and every page. If all goes to check, they will index your website in Google's index. Soon after, your website will be ranked for its targeted keywords.

199. Get Indexed Before Anything Else
If you're starting a website, you'll find that it can take up to three months for the Googlebot to arrive on the scene and crawl your site. Make sure that your website is indexed by following the next few tips.

200. Sign Up For A Google Webmasters Account – It can take up to a month until the Googlebots get to your site.
There is a shortcut to getting indexed quickly in the space of about a week. You need to join Google Webmaster Tools. This is where you can get crawled by the Googlebots and find out if your pages have been indexed. There are a repository of other tools too, which ease the workload of maintaining a healthy, Google-friendly website.

Google Webmasters contains everything you need to make sure your website is fully functioning technically and fulfils all the requirements for crawling and indexing. You'll get full reports on your website including indexing reports, search traffic, keywords sending traffic, linking patterns, updates and more. Google may even send messages to your site on unusual linking patterns or on sharp uptakes in traffic.
(www.google.com/webmasters)

201. Submit URL to Google
Google allow webmasters to submit their URL for inclusion on Google's index. Once submitted, Googlebots will come to your site and crawl it. If all goes well (working technically, good content and no malicious spam), your site will be indexed.
(https://www.google.com/webmasters/tools/submit-url)

202. Check For Crawl Hazards
These are hazards that block Google's spiderbots from crawling and indexing your webpage. Should you have any of these attributes on your pages, they may keep crawlers away and this leads to lower rankings in the long term. Google have said that poor navigability in a website signals no authority or expertise in the area. A poor website probably means a poor user experience.

Avoid the following pitfalls by making sure they aren't included on your website, which are the nest few tips.

203. Flash Can't Be Read By The Googlebot
Google can't read any Flash based webpages. They have become less and less common but are still found. Never use Flash for any part of your webpages because Google cannot read, understand or crawl Flash code. If you built a page entirely on Flash, you might as well have built a white, empty page for all Google cares. To you, it looks like a beautifully designed animated page but to Google, it's a confusing mess that the spiderbots will just label "empty".

204. Password/Form Protected Pages Don't Get Indexed
If a page can only be accessed by filling out a form or entering password, spiderbots cannot access the page. This is an advantage for the majority of pages since you don't want password protected pages ranking on Google anyway. However, just in case there are any protected pages you want indexed, take out the form or link to the page.

205. Javascript Links Are Dodgy
If you've embedded any links on your page in Javascript, Google may not crawl or give any notice of these links. They may not even pass PageRank to other pages. Use HTML instead.

206. See How The Googlebots View Your Page
Think your website looks awesome? Wait until you see what the Googlebots *actually* see. They don't take CSS or Javascript into consideration when crawling your site, since all they see is just the bare HTML elements.

Head over to www.seo-browser.com and input one of your website's URLs. You can see if all your desired elements appear (such as text and images) or if search engines don't see anything at all. It's a real detector that will show you what Google truly sees when it crawls your site. You just might be surprised.

207. Remove Ugly URLs –
There's nothing worse than an ugly URL to ruin a Googlebot's day. They cannot read these URL's or understand what they mean. If keywords are found in a URL, they signify to Google what you are trying to rank for and that your content is relevant to the keywords. Take a look at the following examples of an ugly URL and a friendly URL. For example:

Ugly URL: www.website.com/56shvj3
Friendly URL: www.website.com/technical/googlebot-basics

From a crawler's point of view, the ugly URL looks extremely dodgy and very irrelevant. They cannot understand what the URL means, what keywords it is targeting and what it is about.
The friendly URL on the other hand, is understandable and easy to follow. You'd want to read this, wouldn't you?
Check your pages for any ugly URL's and try to keep them as clean and clutter-free as possible.

208. Merge Multiple URL's Into One
Take a look at the URL's below. They all refer to the homepage of a website. However, notice that every URL is different. Note that whilst they are all pointing to essentially the same page, search engines view them as five separate pages.
1. http://mydomain.com/
2. http://www.mydomain.com/
3. http://www.mydomain.com/default.asp
4. http://mydomain.com/default.asp
5. http://Mydomain.com/Default.asp

This means that Google will view all the pages as duplicates, resulting in a rather unfair slap from Google Panda.

Firstly, check if these pages actually exist. Not all websites have this problem so don't get caught up in a fictional obstacle. Type them into your browser and see if your homepage loads up. If more than one of the links appears, you need to set your default homepage! Simply follow the steps below.
You can solve this mishap by defining a "canonical" link tag in your HTML code. This tag basically tells Google what your default/desired homepage URL is and the URL that you want to load when a searcher clicks on it.

This should clear up any confusion that search engines would have with the URL's. is the code you need to type in to make the fix. Place it directly after the <head/> tag.

```
<link rel="canonical" href="http://example.com" />
```

209. Watch Out For "Printer Friendly" Pages, As They're Duplicates
You don't want duplicate pages on your site. Watch out for any printer-friendly pages that you have on your site because if you update the normal page, you'll have to update the printer friendly pages too. Also, Google only indexes one page of the same content so if your printer friendly page is considered more relevant than the normal page, your visitors will be shown to your no CSS, no Javscript, completely plain printer page. Not good.

Either get rid of printer friendly pages altogether or get them de-indexed by following the tip below.

210. How To Create Printer Friendly Pages By Getting Them De-indexed
If you want to keep your printer friendly pages, you can get them de-indexed by typing the following code into the <head> tag of your page.

```
< meta name="ROBOTS" content="NOINDEX">
```

Once the Googlebots arrive on your site, they'll read the code, drop the page and move on to the next page.
Add the above code to any pages you don't want indexed by Google.

211. Create A Robots.txt File
If you want to block Google from crawling and indexing certain pages (log in or member only pages), you need to create a robots.txt file. This file blocks the Googlebots from crawling that page. You should also create a robots.txt file to block malicious spambots from scanning your website for private data. The best way to create a robots.txt file without coding, is to head over to this link: www.yellowpipe.com/yis/tools/robots.txt

It's the best tool for the job since it blocks over 130 spambots to your website also. Spambots are well-known to scrape email addresses, phone numbers and other private information from websites, so prevention is the key to making sure they don't do damage.

212. Check Your Robots.txt File
Getting your robots.txt file messed up (even one tiny mistake), can prevent crawlers from accessing your site entirely. This tool checks if your robots.txt is functioning correctly and can be read by crawlers (www.frobee.com/robots-txt-check). It's always worth a check, right?

213. Create An XML Sitemap
Sitemaps give crawlers more accessibility, and are one darn useful resource to have.

XML is one difficult language to code in, let me tell you! That's why there are tons of websites that will generate sitemaps for your website. You can use the sitemap creator in Google Webmaster Tools.
Or, head over to www.xml-sitemaps.com to generate your sitemap in minutes.

214. Check Your Sitemap
Again, just like the robotst.txt file, you don't want your sitemap getting botched up. It would be fatal.

Make sure your sitemap is working well and is fully readable. You don't want the Googlebots to get bogged down in your sitemap. Use the sitemap checker in Webmaster Tools or the one here: www.sitemapinspector.com

Simple Ways To Get Your Website Loading Faster

215. You Need A Fast (Or Fairly Fast) Website, Fact
Fast is the new cool. Pages that load at lightning speed have a HUGE advantage over snail speed pages. If you have fast Internet, you may still come across a page that takes minutes to load (or may never load at all). I have come across some websites that have about five HD film-length videos, tons of CSS style sheets, JavaScript animations, a complex website design and about thirty hi-res, super HD images.

According to Aberdeen Group, a 1 second delay in your page load time results in 11% fewer page views, a 7% loss in conversion and a 16% decrease in customer satisfaction.

For Amazon, page load time is an essential part of their business. For every 100 milliseconds improvement in page load time, they report a 1% increase in revenue.

Sure, the more multimedia your page has – well, the better it is. But going overboard often means that many people with medium or slow internet speed will probably never land on your website. Google take PageSpeed very seriously. If you're website is lagging behind, it could face extreme consequences such as lower rankings and it will be a real challenge to get to page one or two, even if you do everything else that's required.

216. Use Google PageSpeed Insights For More Personalized Tips

Luckily, there are a few tips that you can employ to become like lightning. Google find PageSpeed so important that they developed a tool for the job. Head over to https://developers.google.com/speed/pagespeed/insights and input either your website's home page link or the piece of content you want ranking. You will get a score from 1 to 100 with 1 being snail speed and 100 being thunderbolt fast. Striking a balance within the two is key, try aiming for 60-80. You can achieve this by following the personalized tips (tailored to your page) that they have.

217. Get Even More Speed Tips With Pingdom

Here's yet another site that you can effectively use to get more tips for speeding up your site. Whilst I can list out the most common issues that slow down websites, there are always a few issues that aren't so obvious. You might get some great ideas on speeding up your site from this tool. (http://tools.pingdom.com/fpt/)

218. Web Page Test

You might as well get *even more* personalized tips for improving your site speed, right? Here is the third and final website which will check your website's page load time and offer suggestions. It's fast, easy to use and I love it. (www.webpagetest.org)

219. Supercharge Your Site's Speed and Security With CloudFlare

This is probably one of the greatest developments in internet history. CloudFlare makes your site load twice as fast, blocks attackers and uses a Content Delivery Network to allow anyone across the world to access your website in a quicker time. The best part? It's free.

If you want to speed up your website even more, but don't want to pay for extremely expensive hosting, you should give CloudFlare a try. It takes five minutes to set up (literally) and doesn't require any technical expertise at all. I've tried it before and I have found a huge benefit from it. (www.cloudflare.com)

220. Upgrade Your Hosting
If you're paying five to ten dollars for your hosting, don't expect to break any speed records. If you're website is getting over ten thousand visitors a month, it's time to start considering more expensive hosting options. Even an upgrade to twenty dollars a month is enough to get a faster page load time. If you've implemented all the PageSpeed strategies mentioned above, and your website is still taking over 7 seconds to load, you may need to seriously think about upgrading your hosting.

221. Get Rid of HTML "Junk" To Speed Up Time
Check your HTML files and make sure that you get rid of comments, white spaces and anything that doesn't directly impact on your HTML code. This will speed up your page load time a little, and since you don't really need comments and white spaces, you can afford to take them out. You can make a saving of up to 28% on your page load time by "minifying" your CSS and HTML files.

222. Check For Broken Links
Pages come and go, but links are forever.

That's why you need to check for broken links (links that point to pages which no longer exist) on your website. They're a real pain in the backside, from both a UX and technical point of view.
Luckily, you can easily find broken links with Xenu's Link Sleuth (http://bit.ly/1cU7Fmx), for Windows. It needs to be downloaded to your computer and set up properly.

If you're using a Mac, try Integrity instead (www.peacockmedia.co.uk/integrity). Similarly to Xenu's Link Sleuth, it needs to be downloaded to your computer.

223. Compress Your CSS Files

Once you have taken out unnecessary comments out of your HTML and CSS files, it's time to "compress" the files. It takes things to the extreme. Basically, it gets rid of all the "lines" of code, and instead, compresses all the lines into one huge block of code. Yes, it may be hard to read, but it can speed up your site hugely. Compress your CSS files at www.csscompressor.com. Keep a copy of your old CSS file just in case you need to make changes to it in the future. You can always do your edits on your old CSS file (the file that wasn't compressed) and compress it again later.

Whatever you do, make sure to always have a backup copy!

224. Put CSS Files and Javascript Files At The End of Your Code

This at least allows the browser to load up the basic HTML elements and can then download the CSS and Javascript files afterward. This just makes sure that the browser doesn't get stuck on loading up a Javascript file, and risks the user leaving the page completely.

225. Compress Your Image

Compression reduces the size of an image without degrading the quality of the image to an unacceptable level. It basically converts the image to binary code and looks for patterns in the code. If it finds recurring patterns, it compresses these patterns into one pattern. Make sure that all your images are compressed. This will greatly improve your site's page load time.

226. Use Image Compression Tools

There are three image compression tools which I recommend. There are two types of image compression tools; web based tools and local tools. Web based image compression tools offer less customization than local tools, but are quicker and easier to use. Local image compression gives you more functionality and allows you to customize other

Here is a list of the best local and web-based image compression tools:

Web-based Image Compression Tools
- Yahoo! Smush.It – www.smushit.com/ysmush.it
- TinyPNG – www.tinypng.org

Local Image Compression Tools (Need To Be Downloaded)

- ImageOptim – www.imageoptim.com – For Mac only – JPEG, PNG and GIF
- Caesium – www.caesium.sourceforge.net – For Windows only – PNGs, BMP and JPG
- JStrip – www.davidcrowell.com/jstrip - For Windows only - JPEG

227. Use External Javascript Files

Javascript is a lot of code to digest. Trying to download all that Javascript code on every page can really slow things down. Use external Javascript files just like your CSS files, and link them to the HTML file. That way, if the user triggers the need for Javascript code – the file will kick into action. It's a lot better than downloading the code every time, when users mightn't even need to use it.

228. Flash Should Get The Boot

Sorry, folks but if your website is using Flash for animation, it's being slowed down completely. That, and the Googlebot can't read the code properly either. Just take out your Flash completely and get rid of it. Or else, use it in very tiny amounts when absolutely necessary.

229. Don't Use More Than One Analytics Program

Using five analytics programs? Every time you need to embed tracking code into your website, you are slowing it down. You really don't need more than two analytics programs. Google Analytics contains pretty much everything you need and provides all the advanced functionality that other analytics programs have.

If you feel the need to use another analytics program as well as GA, you may have enough leeway to do this. However, do not exceed trying to embed more than two tracking codes because you will seriously slow down your website.

230. Watch The Number of Videos You Have Per Page

Whilst one video or even two videos don't slow down your page drastically, make sure to keep an eye on the number of videos you have per page. For example, your Home Page is essentially a landing page for potential customers. Let's say you add a video to it that contains customer testimonials. If a video will slow down your page even by a few hundred milliseconds, it's still precious time. Instead, use videos on pages where you don't rely so heavily on converting searchers into customers.

Mobile Optimization

231. Use The TouchSwipe JQuery Plug-In

Optimize for certain mobile manoeuvres such as swipe, zoom and pinch. If users can't do these seemingly simple tasks on your website, you could lose them. Google will also be checking for this when ranking your site. You can optimize your site for this by installing the TouchSwipe JQuery plug-in.

232. Get Responsive

A mobile-friendly site means that it changes the desktop site to become mobile-friendly by enlarging text, shifting the grid around to make sure all the elements fit together and making buttons larger. It uses the same content as a desktop website, so it isn't a duplicate of the desktop website.

Basically, it's the same website but it changes slightly for a mobile device. It also alters to different mobile devices such as tablets or smaller mobile devices. So the website would appear differently on an iPhone than on an iPad.

You can either make your website responsive or make a separate mobile website (when a mobile device gets to the website it is redirected to the mobile website). If you want to take Google's word for it, they recommend a responsive website. Also, it makes things easier since you don't have an entirely separate website to look after.

233. Don't Create A Separate Mobile Domain
Many businesses go mobile by creating a separate mobile domain by using the "m-dot" technique, eg: www.m.mydomain.com. I strongly advise against this, for the sole reason that trying to maintain two separate websites is a nightmare. When you publish a blog post on your desktop website, you always need to remember to publish it to the mobile site.

Any small changes you make on the desktop website will have to be done on the mobile website too. As you can see, this provides you with nothing but more work and less time for other activities.

234. Use Icons Instead of Text Buttons
When you want to include buttons in your website such as in Call To Actions and navigation bar buttons, use icons instead of text. So instead of the "Home" text button in the navigation bar, you could use an icon of a home instead.

This is very simple but is a technique that will bring user experience to an all-time high. Going mobile is all about taking out the noise and bringing out the best in your website.

235. No Zooming Should Be Required
Design your mobile friendly website in such a way that no zooming should be required to view your text or buttons. Text size should be a minimum of 16 pixels, if you want it to be easily read.

236. Don't Cluster Buttons Together
Users can make a lot of misplaced clicks when you have a lot of buttons clustered together. When they select one button, a nearby button may be clicked instead. Make sure that your buttons are spaced out evenly, making it easier for users to select the right button. Also, keep buttons as large as possible. There's nothing more infuriating for mobile UX than a bunch of tiny buttons.

237. When Going Mobile, Keep Things Simple
There's no need to get too complex on the design of your mobile website. Retain the navigation bar, sidebar and on-page content. But there's no need to include too many flashy features, because a mobile screen is small and can't hold all the space that a typical desktop can. Simplicity is also the key to a quick page load time.

238. Avoid Flash, Frames and PNG-24 Formats
These nasty additions to your mobile site could result in some nasty user experiences. Since most smartphones and tablets can't play Flash or frames, it would be dumb to go including them. You can use HTML5, CSS, jQuery, JPG and GIF files for your mobile site, which all work perfectly on a mobile device.

239. Don't Use Pop Ups
Mobile phones don't have the same leverage as a desktop, so remember – no pop ups. It's common sense really, but just in case you migrated your desktop to mobile, you may have brought the popups too.

240. Don't Delay On Going Mobile, It's Urgent
Google have their April 21st mobile algorithm change, they've convinced practically every webmaster as part of their #MobileMarch campaign and more than half of all web traffic is through a mobile device. You need to go mobile, and fast. Sites without a mobile friendly site will face penalties and lower rankings as a result.

241. Take The Mobile Friendly Test
How mobile friendly is your website? Are you doing enough or is your site still lagging behind? Get these answers and more from the experts themselves, Google. Simply input your website URL and get the results! Do the test at: www.google.com/webmasters/tools/mobile-friendly/

242. Use The "Click To Call Feature"
Want someone to give you a phone call? By placing a "Click To Call" button on your site, people can ring you immediately if they have questions or want to become a customer.

This is probably the only feature that is specific to mobile devices only, and can only be used if you have a separate mobile website domain. If you use responsive site, you cannot use this feature. Also, you'll only need to use this feature if you have a local business and want to get customers for your business.

243. Make It Local, If You're A Business
Enhance the whole "local" aspect to your website for mobile devices. Include your mobile phone number, a click to call button, address and opening hours. Research has proven that over 50% of mobile searchers are to get more information about a local business or company. Make sure to optimize for this, by having all your business details ready.

Also, incorporate rich snippets such as your phone number and join Google My Business. This will give you an entire section in the SERPs if someone searches your company's name. Details such as your opening hours, phone number, map with location and review stars are all included as part of the Google My Business feature. You'll find more on this in Chapter 7.

244. Make It Easy For Someone To Share
Research has found that 72% of Facebook users use it on a mobile device. Many websites are not optimizing for this by abandoning social share buttons completely. Make sure they are either at the top or bottom of the page, or *somewhere*. When 72% of your potential audience are using a mobile device, there's no reason why you shouldn't be optimizing for this.

245. Minimize The Number of Share Buttons You Use
Keep your social sharing buttons to a bare minimum. You seriously don't need social sharing buttons for Digg or Stumble Upon because chances are, if someone wants to share your content – they're probably on Facebook, Twitter or Pinterest already.

Having more than six social sharing buttons really starts to slow things down big time. Also, that's not to mention the sheer ugliness all those social buttons create. Keep it to four social sharing buttons maximum, and no more than that.

246. Get All The Tech Specs With Screaming Frog

When you're checking if your website has all the necessary technical requirements (proper redirects, on-page SEO, links working and so on), you need Screaming frog. Download it at www.screamingfrog.co.uk/seo-spider/

This crawls your entire site and grabs data on pages, links, page titles, redirects, 404s, heading tags, status codes, attribute lengths, anchor text, alt text and numbers of internal back links, numbers of external links and so much more. You can also download all the data into Excel, and check on it then.

CHAPTER 7
Local SEO

If you have a local business that needs more customers, you can use these tips to get started with the basics of Local SEO. Whilst they aren't extensive and are not advanced Local SEO strategies, they will still put you ahead of other competitor websites.

247. Get Your Business Listed On Google
You need to get your business listed on Google. This is the first part of your local SEO strategy. This will require you to fill in basic details about your site such as opening hours, contact details and location. It will then build a page about your business based on the information you give. This page will then rank in search results. So, when someone searches for "dentist denver" or "dentist near me", your page on Google My Business will rank. Get your business page at www.google.com/business today.

248. Check If Your Business Is Listed With Its Phone Number
Sometimes, one of your colleagues may have gotten your business listed with Google already. Always check beforehand since Google discourages duplicate listings of the same business, and a mistake like that could ban you from getting listed entirely.

You may want to check if your business is listed already, but don't search for your business name. Google only provides exact match results, so if the name isn't exactly right, it won't show up in the results. Instead, search for your business's phone number on Google Places. Since your phone number is unique only to your business, no other businesses will show up.

249. Add The 'Local Business' Rich Snippet
You can also optimize for search results by including a "local business" rich snippet on your website. This rich snippet will contain all kinds of juicy data such as contact details, location and opening hours. Go to www.schema-creator.org and select the Local Business Rich Snippet. Then, fill it out with all the details of your business. Get the generated HTML code and paste it into your website!

Once you have that done, you need to check if the rich snippets are working. Go to Google's rich snippet (also known as structured data) testing tool at www.developers.google.com/structured-data/testing-tool/ and paste in your URL once you've clicked on the "Fetch as URL" button.

250. Get Reviews
The next step to getting your local SEO on the road to successful, is to get positive reviews on your page, and lots of them. These reviews will show to Google that your business is doing an excellent job and that your business can easily be trusted. Trust equals more customers in the search engine world. If Google thinks your business is more trustworthy and does its job better than competitors, it will drive more searchers to your business by ranking you first.

251. Generate The URL To Write Reviews On Your Business Page
Firstly, before you go asking people to review your business service, you need to generate the URL to do so.
The problem with just sending them the link of your page is that they will have to navigate through the page to find the reviews section. It's very tedious for them, and could result in less conversion. Instead, you can generate a URL which loads up your business page, and cause a pop up to appear which asks them to review your business.

Get the URL of your business page on Google My Business. Then, remove the "/posts" part of the URL. Paste the following snippet into the end of the URL:
```
/?hl=en&review=1
```

252. Print The QR Code To Submit Review On Business Cards
Rather than using your default business cards which have your contact information, you can create a new set of business cards which are only related to getting the review on your business page. First, get your URL for your business page that has a review pop up (see above). Then, generate a QR code by using www.qrstuff.com.

What I love about this tool is that it allows you to change the colour of your QR code, meaning you can add your website logo to the QR code. Print this QR code on your business card, and also, add an incentive or free discount if they write their review (see below).

253. Send Past Customers A Link To Review

Write an email asking all your past customers and clients to write a quick review of you on Google. You can offer them a discount for future purchases, if they write an honest review. You can also give them a phone call, and ask them to write a review. Whatever it is, make sure all your past customers are asked to write a review!

254. Offer Discounts/Incentives For Readers To Write A Review

There's a difference between paying them to write a review and asking them to write an honest review in exchange for a voucher or extra incentive. Provided their review is unbiased, totally honest, I wouldn't think there is anything wrong with doing this. Reviews are hard to come by lately, and if an incentive will get them to review, it's well worth your time.

Maybe you could offer them a $10 discount voucher for their next purchase or a free gift that's paid by you. Whatever it is, make sure it isn't too expensive as you don't want that eating into your budget!
Also, emphasise on an *honest* review. Mention to them that just because they received something from you, doesn't mean they have to write a perfect, five star review. Tell them that whatever negative points they have will be taken as constructive feedback and will be worked on in the future.

255. Add Review Stars To Your Website Too

Don't ignore adding review stars on your website either. Getting reviews from the Google My Business Page isn't the only way to get reviews!
By adding review stars, your website will stick out hugely in search results as well as the Google My Business Page listing too. That's killing two birds with the one stone! Once you get a couple of reviews on your website, you won't need anymore. The rest of your "review getting" efforts will have to go into the Google My Business Page.

256. Use Photos In Your Google My Business Page

Very few businesses and companies are actually using the photos section of the "My Business" Page. The last time I've seen an image in a business listing is a couple of months ago at least.

Images are what will attract more customers. They don't just want a map of your business location, they want to see what your office looks like or the products you provide. Maybe, you could provide an image of your service in action! That would really look exciting!

A few simple images can really improve click through rates and set you apart from the other businesses ranking for your keyword.

257. Get The Opening Hours Right

You'd be very surprised at how many people get the opening hours wrong. I've seen a lot of listings on Google which said they were closed in the morning, when clearly they were opened. Since so many people are checking opening hours of companies through Google now, you could really lose out if you get your opening hours wrong. Pay attention when you're inputting the opening hours into the listing.

Also, do a check now and again by searching for your business on Google, and check the opening hours.

258. Insert Geographic Keywords In Your H1 Tag, And Content

If you're targeting a certain area such as Brighton in the UK, you need to insert the keyword "brighton" in your title tag, h1 tag and content for optimization. Many companies have seen jumps of three to six pages just by including geographic keywords on their pages. Obviously, there's no need to include these keywords in blog posts and infographics, but for your main "sales or information" pages, you'll need to include the keywords there.

259. Target Your Regular Keywords Too

Don't forget about targeting your regular keywords too! For example, if you have a pizza delivery service, make sure you include the keyword "pizza delivery" or "delivering pizza" in your title. That way, when you mesh the geographic keywords and regular keywords together, you get something like the following as your title tag:

Pizza Company X | Delivering Pizza To Chicago

260. Build Citations

A citation is an online reference to your business' name, address and phone number, without actually including a link to your site. Similar to backlinks, Google count the number of quality citations your business gets and ranks you accordingly.

This is an example of a citation:
Name of Business, 99 Links Street, City, Region, Post Code (Phone Number)

Your citation should be exactly as named on your Google My Business page. Don't change the business name around or the arrangement of the address. Everything has to be the exact same as what's on your page.
You can build citations through:
- Industry specific directories
- Guest posts
- Profile pages
- Forum and Q&A signatures
- Video and SlideShare descriptions

A lot of the linkbuilding techniques that are covered can also be applied to building citations. Instead of adding a backlink to your site, you can add a citation to your business instead.
You can also find the best places to get citations with this nifty tool:
www.whitespark.ca/local-citation-finder

261. Get Listed On Other Sites
Get listed on Yelp and Yahoo Local as part of your local SEO strategy. Again, these sites will require you to fill out all the basic but essential information about your business such as opening hours, contact and location. These sites will provide a lot of link juice back to your site.

262. What Factors Will Boost Your Website In The Local Search Results?
The number of reviews, number of citations and how positive your reviews are overall, are the main factors which will determine your local search ranking. By continuing to work on these, you can really boost your website's ranking in local search results.

You need to keep getting a couple of reviews and citations every month, and keep the stream slow but steady. You don't want a huge spike in reviews over a week, and then receive none for the next six months. Also, make sure that you have optimized for geographic keywords by including them on your website's homepage and sales page.

263. Don't Buy Reviews, You'll Get Into Deep Trouble
Don't start getting black hat with local SEO. Buying reviews from others is a sure-fire black hat SEO technique. It's never going to work. Just like buying links and getting penalized, Google will stamp down on your reviews.

They have intelligence beyond your wildest dreams.
For example, if they saw two five star reviews written in New York about a flower arranging service in Brighton, UK – things would start to look ugly. Unless the person writes the review in your local area, there is no chance for paid reviews to work. So just get them naturally, through the methods I've outlined above.

264. Should You Keep Working On Local SEO? – Compared to the likes of normal SEO where you have to keep chugging away at it, local SEO can be done and then put on the backburner for a while. After all, once you get listed, add your rich snippets, get a few citations, optimize for geographic keywords and get some reviews, you're pretty much set for success.

However, I don't mean you stop your local SEO *entirely.* You still have to get a stream of reviews and citations every two months, just to keep your business relevant and looking up to date. If you continually ask new customers to write reviews and get some citations from local websites, your local SEO is sorted for that month anyway.

CHAPTER 8
Predictions For 2020

What will SEO look like in 2020? How can you start preparing for the change? Here are some predictions for what SEO will look like in 2020. It's only a few years away, so make sure to start preparing for it today! Keep in mind though that these predictions aren't 100% accurate. Take them with a pinch of salt. After all, I'm not psychic.

265. Semantic Search Will Take Hold

Today, semantic search is only at its infancy. It's nothing but a baby.

Wait until 2020 (or even better, 2050) and you'll see semantic search flexing its muscles for real.
Expect a lot more functionality from the Knowledge Graph, and scarily good responses to your searches. Semantic search will know everything about its users and I'd go so far to say that semantic search will understand your brain and personality better than anyone else.

266. Mobile Search Will Become More Dominant

Mobile search is going to become a lot more popular as the years go on. I would go as far to say that mobile search will almost take over desktop search in 2020, but not fully. Desktop search will still be used in the next few years, or even decades so don't let that worry you. However, I think that the use of mobile search is going to rapidly increase, exponentially.

267. Local Search Will Become More Important

People search Google for things like their nearest restaurant, phone numbers of local businesses or opening hours of shops. This is going to increase even more in 2020

268. Google Will Start Pulling Answers From Your Content

People don't want to scroll through a list of websites in search results. They don't want to click on a website link and wait for it load. They want the answer, there and then. Instantly.

That's why Google are "pulling" the answers from the schema markup of website content. For example, if you type in searches like "walt disney's birthday", "what is the sun", "what does serendipity mean", "what time is it", you get answers instantly straight from Google. They pull these answers from other websites and may provide attribution to the source.

But it's not just one word answers. You can now get full length answers for queries like "symptoms of stroke" or "how to stay healthy" which have entire paragraphs. Those paragraphs are pulled straight from other blogs. It's very unfair, and stops a lot of traffic from reaching the site.
This new product of Google is called the "Google Answer Box" (no surprises there). Expect it to become more and more intelligent. By 2020, it'll have answers to practically everything and anything.

269. Those That'll Translate Their Content Will Win
Most online content is in English, with very little actually being translated into other languages. This is saying something, since the two most spoken languages in the world are Mandarin and Spanish. Then, it's English.

With rising populations across the world, by 2020, the audience for your writing will be *huge.*
If you want more readers, it really helps to start translating content into those languages.
It's simple. Those that'll translate their content will get a huge increase in traffic over anyone else.

You need to invest in getting your content translated because by 2020, a lot more webmasters will be doing the same. You might even discover that a lot of your target audience is in other countries. Some of the most successful companies have the most users in South America and Asia.
It helps to get your content translated. So, start now. If you want to postpone it now, make sure you start translating in the next few years. It's got to be happen soon.

270. There'll Be More Rich Snippets

Rich snippets are hot and as they're working incredibly well, Google are going to keep on using them. By 2020, they are definitely going to create more rich snippets. I can't say what, but I know they're on the pipeline. Make sure to prepare for new rich snippets by using the rich snippets already available, and reading the latest news on SEO blogs (Search Engine Land, Search Engine Watch, Moz).

271. Google Panda Will Perform In Real-Time

Google actually have to refresh their Panda and Penguin algorithms regularly to keep the spam sites down and bring up the high quality sites. That means every few months, they have to hit a "refresh" button and release Panda and Penguin again.

However, one Google engineer hinted that Panda now performs in real-time, meaning it's working around the clock and no matter when, it'll always deliver high quality results. This statement was later dismissed as another Google engineer said it was not true. Panda may not be working in real-time today, but in the future it most certainly will.

By 2020, I'm certain that Panda and Penguin will both work simultaneously in real-time to deliver the best results no matter when. Even today, we've almost reached that near-intelligence and it doesn't seem to long away when these two algorithm updates will always run.

272. Social Media Will Become A Ranking Signal

Sometime, somewhere down the line – social media signals will have to become a ranking factor. They are already part of the ranking algorithm, but aren't considered important. Google have tried incorporating Facebook and Twitter signals into their algorithm, but it was a disaster.

However, I wouldn't be surprised if they were still working on it. After all, social media and Google are now intertwined. If something is popular on social media, it has to be popular on Google.

273. Trust Will Become More Important

As Google learned their lessons from websites that manipulated them, they have put more emphasis on the trust with the website. Things like comments on content, subscribers, and high quality links all build trust. Building trust is one of the most difficult things to do in SEO, because there are no tricks or quick hacks that you can use to get there.

The only way you can build trust is by creating awesome content that people enjoy, providing an excellent user experience and getting links and mentions from reputable websites. Getting and becoming all that is difficult, no doubt, but is achievable in the years to come.

Of course, when you build trust, Google may even rank you higher in the future, just because they recognise your brand and know you will do a great job for their searchers. Expect trust to become even more powerful than it is today.

274. Online Identity Will Continue To Become Stronger

– Just like trust, online identity will prove to be big. Do you know why Mashable, Buzzfeed, Forbes and The Huffington Post continue to rank extremely well for competitive keywords? They've earned Google's trust and became an online identity.

Whilst it's unlikely that your website will become a massive empire like theirs, you can still build a strong online identity in your niche through powerful link building, content marketing and providing value to searchers.

Don't think you need a massive advertising team worth millions of dollars to build an identity either. Take Brian Dean's SEO blog, Backlinko which was built 12 months ago and has 24 blog posts. That's it. This blog is now one of the most popular and reputable SEO blogs on the web, and it was all made possible by one person. All he did was provide insane value to his readers, build powerful backlinks and create content which Google took a shine to.

275. HTTPS Will Be Essential To Any Business Driven Website – Google have already started to push for "HTTPS" websites (not just your regular http:// website but one that's extra secure and is called https:// instead). In 2015, it has become a ranking factor and I will suspect that for commerce and sites that involve monetary transactions, getting a HTTPS site will be a big deal. By 2020, it will be almost compulsory for most sites to have a HTTPS site. However, for purely informational sites that involve no monetary transactions, getting a HTTPS site won't be so important.

276. Google+ Will Die – I'm sorry, but I *had* to say it.
Google take +1's from their own social network very seriously, and so if you have a lot of +1's on your content, you may get an ever so tiny boost in the rankings. However, their failed attempt at Google+ is going to come to an end someday. They mightn't "end" Google+ officially, but they will turn it from a product to a platform. They will get rid of any ties that Google+ has with either paid search or organic search results.
The ingenious products that are available on Google+ such as Hangouts will continue, but maybe not in the social network that we know of today.

277. Search Results Will Contain Specific Content, Not Broad Content – Search queries on Google are getting longer, with lots of queries reaching up to eight and nine words. It's inevitable that search results will get even more specific as time goes on. So rather than ranking search results that provide a broad overview of the topic, Google will put more emphasis on sites that answer the search query directly and specifically.

278. Google Will Continue To Remove Data From Analytics – Ever since Google took out the keywords that people used to find your site from Google Analytics, and replaced them with [not provided], there was out roar among SEOs.
It's still debatable on why Google removed this feature. Maybe because they wanted to protect their searcher's privacy (which is more than likely). Or some of the pessimists say that Google don't want SEOs to succeed. By removing the feature, SEOs couldn't discover which keywords were sending them traffic and hence, optimize their site for those keywords even more.

CHAPTER 8: PREDICTIONS FOR 2020

Google have taken keywords from Google Webmasters which means that for a lot of the keywords in Google Webmaster Tools, they will show up as "not provided". This is not good news for any webmaster, and it's only going to get worse in the future.

Google don't want SEOs succeeding, because to them, SEO is a form of manipulation. Yes, I agree.

SEO *can* be a form of manipulation, but only if your website provides no value to your readers. SEO will continue to be the number one form of marketing, and there's no way that Google can stop it. They'll keep picking away at SEOs though, so by 2020, expect to have some of your favourite SEO features removed.

CHAPTER 9

Content Marketing

Content marketing is all about creating content in the form of infographics, blog posts or videos which rank for keywords and searcher queries on Google. It basically answers any questions searchers may have, or will teach them how to do something. Without content marketing, you'll find it difficult to build lots of search traffic to your site. By creating content, you can easily build lots of traffic and convert that traffic into customers. When people become enchanted by your content, they'll also become enchanted by both **you** and **your business.**

Here are some very inspiring and slightly startling statistics on content marketing:

1. Businesses that blog more than 20 times a month get 5 times more traffic than those who blog less than 4 times a month.
2. Websites that blog get 97% more inbound links than those without.
3. Most people regularly read and follow 5-10 blogs.
4. Websites with blogs get 55% more traffic than those without.

Creating A Magnetic, Viral Title

279. Create An Awesome Title – If you want to become popular online or get traffic or improve your SEO, you need to create an awesome title. It will be an essential process to gaining clicks, traffic and customers.

280. What has Writing Titles Got To Do With SEO?
Writing titles is more of a conversion process or content marketing process, so you may be wondering what it has got to do with SEO.

You need to get links from influencers. An awesome title will increase your chances of snagging the link.

CHAPTER 9: CONTENT MARKETING

You need searchers to click on your search result, not anyone else's. Again, a click worthy title will drive searchers to your result, and no one else's. Writing titles may seem like a silly practice when it comes to SEO, but in this content driven world, titles are the key to a successful website when coupled with content.

281. Include A Number In Your Title, For List Posts
People love numbers, it's just the way it is. The first thing I do when optimizing my titles is adding a number to the beginning, if possible. If you are writing anything in the form of a list, make sure to add a number. The larger the number, the more clicks you will get.

It is just one of those things that you cannot afford to isolate yourself from, just check any article from a major website with a lot of know-how (BuzzFeed, Mashable or HubSpot) and you will find that nearly always, they start with a number.

282. Adding Numbers: Don't Include The Word, Keep It As A Numeral
Remember to include the number as a numeral, rather than a word. You'd be surprised at how many people make this fatal mistake and lose out as a result.

283. Add Power Words
I call these power words because they will really strengthen your title. People take a liking to certain words that evoke strong emotions in them. Research by Buffer shows that the following words will make your title more clickable and will cause a lot of people to read it. Here they are:
Smart/Surprising, History, Hacks, Huge/Big, Critical, Science
If you have an opportunity to use them, just don't think about it. Use. Them.

284. Heighten The Curiosity With Question Marks And The Unexpected
We all are curious people. By including some "mysterious" elements to your title, you can easily draw in more readers. This is especially good for tutorials, where ranking on Google is more difficult for that phrase, so you decide to take the social media route instead.
1) Questions tend to rank well on Google. The best words to use at the beginning of a question title are, "How do I?" "Which?" "What?" and "How?"

Eg: *How do I Start A Kick-Ass Coin Collection?*
Which Country Has The Most Good-Looking People?
What Happens When You Eat Leather?
Why Your Blog May Be Losing Out On Potential Readers

2) Adding an unexpected twist at the end – something strange, wacky or just downright crazy is a fantastic way to engage interest and you could be on the road to viral. Just check this title out (from moz.com):

How I Got The Attention of one of the Top SEO Bloggers With Diet Coke

Isn't that just a great title because of the "diet coke" at the end? I would definitely read that, because it sparked my curiosity. As a side note, that got 77 thumbs up.

The example titles above also have unexpected twists at the end, such as "good looking people" and "leather". For the second title you would expect, the best healthcare system or the highest IQ but good looking people? Now that was unexpected!

285. Brag About The Benefits – A lot of readers think *"What's in it for me?"* just when they are about to click on your link. That's why you need to make it loud and clear: what are the benefits of your content? People need to get sold when they read your title. Your content deserves an awesome title so you need to tell them what they will get if they take the time to read it. There are plenty of ways to do so by including numbers and powerful adjectives.

When we want to learn to get more traffic on Google, seeing a link which says *"20 Ways To Increase Your Traffic from Google: A Beginners Guide"*, we inevitably click on it. This is because the greatness of your article is being reflected onto the title when you say "20" and "a beginners guide".
Here are some words you can use to do just that:

- **How To** – They will learn something new.
- **A Beginner's Guide to** – We are all beginners at something, so a simpler guide will be needed by a lot.
- **10 Ways to…** - Numbers, yet again!

- **Find out how….** – Reader will learn something exclusive, an insider's account etc.
- **Introducing** – Implies something "new", "latest", "fresh"
- **A Simple Formula to** – A quick strategy, or easy instructions to doing a certain task.

286. Emote, Exaggerate and Excite

To get that definitive "click!", you need to do one last thing and excite the reader. Twitter reported that tweets or blog titles with adverbs got more re-tweets than those without. That's because people read on emotion and therefore, you need to appeal to their heart and soul. This can be done with adverbs, all caps, an unexpected twist, asterisks, exclamation points and flash words. Exaggerating and being **bold** works too.

- **Adverbs** – Add in some emotive language with adjectives and adverbs. Consult a thesaurus for original ones, but a good bloggers list includes: viral, epic, free, amazingly, life-changing, unexpected, irresistibly, mind-blowing, mistakenly.
- **Be bold** – Use some exaggerative language (but only if your blog post is deserving of this title). For example, "Kick-Ass", "Change Your Life", "Extinction", "Kill", "War". Tabloid newspaper language uses a lot of these words; and I now know why they have such a following. Eg: Microsoft *Kill the Windows XP: Why this Shocking Decision?*
- **Punctuation:** Exclamation points, asterisks, arrows and all caps work wonders but use sparingly!

287. Remember That Shorter is Better

The shorter you can make your title whilst still delivering the goods to your reader, the more people will have the time to read it.

Long, tiring and extraneous (even reading silently in your head) titles have the same effect as if you are reading them aloud. You need to take a huge breath before you read the title. If you have a working title, there may be ways to make it a little shorter.

For example:

That Will –> That'll

These 20 –> 20

Cut out any extraneous words (underlined below), eg: *"How To Make Delicious, Mouth-wateringly Tasty yet Simple Cupcakes That Everyone Will Enjoy Eating"* should become *"How to Make Deliciously Simple Cupcakes That They'll Love"*

288. Use Some of These Sample Headlines

Generating viral headlines can become tiring especially when you try to combine all of the elements above. That's why you can start using the following headlines below. All you have to do is fill in the blanks with your own niche topics/targeted keywords and you are ready to begin!

289. How to [keywords]

I know, this headline is a little generic but when creating headlines, you always have to start simple. This example is the classic headline that will always save you should you become completely stumped on what to write about. It *is* Google's friend, since all articles with this headline are going to rank on Google no matter what. If you don't know where to start, write with a simple "how to" headline.

How to Make an Authentic Christmas Card

How to Use Photoshop (A Technophobe's Guide)

How To Train A Dog To Sit

How To Identify Profitable Keywords for SEO

290. How to [action] (Even If [Obstacle])

Now this one is smart. You're tapping into the "been there, done that" audience who tried to do something but it failed.

Most people have tried to lose weight, for example. They read thousands of articles that guarantee the formula to losing weight, but these promising articles never help.

They just offer the same old stuff with diets…blah, blah that honestly, no one can stick to.

CHAPTER 9: CONTENT MARKETING

Or maybe your audience wants to obtain a certain thing but are unable to do so because of their circumstances. Examples include not being able to do online trading because they aren't good with computers or not able to paint because they just don't have the talent.

How To Lose Weight (Even If You Hate Diets)
How To Paint Like Picasso (Even If You Never Painted A Thing In Your Life)
How To Make A Household Budget (Even If You're Not Good With Numbers)

291. 9 Lies [Your Niche] Experts Like To Tell

This one appeals to the fears of your readers. Lies? Experts? It gets them palpitating even before they read your post.

9 Lies SEO Experts Like To Tell
10 Lies Teachers Like To Tell About Your Kid
16 Lies Google Like To Tell About SEO

292. 6 Little-Known Factors That Could Affect Your [Activity]

This also arouses some curiosity within the reader and gets them thinking. Everyone wants to improve what they do, and always want to learn the pitfalls that could be pulling them down.

12 Little-Known Factors That Could Affect Your PageSpeed
9 Little-Known Factors That Could Affect Your Examination Performance
15 Little-Known Factors That Could Affect Your Blood Sugar Levels

293. 8 [Your Niche] Mistakes You Don't Know You're Making

Ouch. This has got to hurt. These mistakes aren't your average "know them already" mistakes. They are mistakes that everyone is making…but don't even realize it.

This title is going to ignite huge curiosity in your readers, both on Google and social media.

9 SEO Mistakes You Don't Know You're Making
13 Fashion Mistakes You Don't Know You're Making
7 Blog Post Mistakes You Don't Know You're Making

294. How To [Activity] – The Definitive Guide

This title sets the mark. It's going to cover every little detail about a particular topic and it's going to be awesome. No other article will ever come *near* the standard of this. These are the articles that garner the most attention because Google will love them. People will get talking about your guide and how it sets your niche to a whole new ballgame.

How To Do A TED Talk – The Definitive Guide

How To Create A Killer Slideshare – The Definitive Guide
How To Do Technical SEO – The Definitive Guide
You are promising your readers something spectacular, so don't use this title unless you're willing to put in the work.

295. 25 [Resources/Tricks] That'll Instantly Make You A Better [Person]
Simply list out the tips and tools you use on a day to day basis and give a small description on each one. Make sure to give the resources a hyperlink and you're all set! There'll be plenty of bookmarks and social media shares for this title!
25 Resources That'll Instantly Make You A Better Writer
21 Resources That'll Instantly Make You A Better Web Designer
18 Tricks That'll Instantly Make You A Better Guitarist

296. 11 Ways To Completely Revamp Your [Activity/Object]
Did you just say, revamp? Revamp equals "better", "anew" and other feel-good words. It ignites a sense of success and will bring back the feeling that hope is not lost.
11 Ways To Completely Revamp Your Website Design
12 Ways To Completely Revamp Your Study Timetable
16 Ways To Completely Revamp Your Kitchen

297. 10 Things Everyone Hates About [Your Niche]
This title signals some light hearted fun about your niche. Make it as funny as possible. Try using the words "memes", "GIFs" and "comics" in the title too.
10 Things Everyone Hates About Wednesdays [In Memes]
10 Things Everyone Hates About Social Media
15 Things Everyone Hates About Their Laptop [With Comics]

298. [Activity]: 12 Do's and Don'ts For Success
We all want success. Do's and don'ts are extremely popular these days, so it's time to follow the crowd.
Going Viral: 12 Do's and Don'ts For Success
Planting Fuschias: 11 Do's and Don'ts For Success
Birdwatching: 21 Do's and Don'ts For Success

299. An Introduction To [Topic]

This title is for all the beginners out there, who cannot understand what the heck it's all about. When we embark on a new hobby we know little about, we tend to research it online first. That's where your article comes in!

An Introduction To Social Media Marketing
An Introduction To Choosing Anti-Virus Software
An Introduction To Writing Science Fiction Novels

300. The Worst Advice You Could Ever Get About [Topic]

Perfect for the "Tell me! Tell me!" effect. Use for unstoppable curiosity.

The Worst Advice You Could Ever Get About Interviews
The Worst Advice You Could Ever Get About Interior Design
The Worst Advice You Could Ever Get About Cooking

301. 10 Tips For Making A Good [Whatever] Even Better

Add fuel to the already burning fire. Add even more momentum to the exponential progress. This takes it to the next level.

10 Tips For Making A Good Website Even Better
15 Tips For Making A Good Soup Even Better
11 Tips For Making A Good SEO Campaign Even Better

302. The [Celebrity/Company] Guide To [Activity]

Whatever niche you're in, there is an inspiring person or company out there who do what they do like a boss. They are the best in their niche, and have a massive following. Who wants to be like them? All of us!

The Steve Jobs Guide To Design
The Oprah Winfrey Guide To Leading A Zen Life
The Pixar Guide To Animation
The Tiger Woods Guide To Golf

303. How To Get Amazing Titles Through Other Blogs
Go to some of the most well-known websites out there such as Buzzfeed, Mashable, Wired and HubSpot (for marketers). Look at some of their titles and see which titles you want to click on. Those are the titles you should be aiming to include on your website. Don't copy the titles, but get inspiration from them. Change a few things around in the title, and add in your own targeted keywords to make a fantastic sounding title.

304. Don't Choose The Boring Title
Writing predictably viral titles is difficult. At Buzzfeed, they conjure about 30 amazing titles per article and choose which one they think will perform best. It's true that writing a title can be a tiresome and aggravating process. After all, the title is what will make or break that piece of content.

It can be tempting to go down the easy route, and just write the title that first pops into your head. Unless you've worked for a content marketing agency, that title is more than likely going to be a little boring, and lacks that "something special" it needs to be popular.

Write a few titles using the strategies above and think about which works best.

305. Don't Go From "Awesome Title" To "Clickbait" – Does clickbait sound familiar? Annoying internet ads, no?
Clickbait is a form of headline writing that leads to a poor quality or spam page, which offers little value to you. Do any of these headlines look familiar?

Stop Putting On Weight, By Eating This One Food!
How Using Facebook Can Earn You Thousands A Day
Learn How Mom Makes $2000 Per Day At Home

Not the best headlines, right? If you've ever clicked on these ads, they only lead you to a virus filled, sales page that requires you to pay hundreds to access the "one weird tip" or the trick "to take twenty years off your face". They may generate tons of clicks, but they don't look like the headlines you'd want on your blog. Most online users have already become immune to these "too good to be true" titles and will only label your website as a piece of spam.

Types of Content You Should Create

306. The Article, or Blog Post
The most common of all, an article is the most basic form of content. Used by millions of bloggers across the world, you can bet that this content is the easiest to create and that doesn't mean you have to be a skilled writer.

People want answers, not stories. They don't care about your writing style or narrative. All they want is the information presented to them in an engaging and educational way.

307. Infographic: A Visual Representation Of Data
This content does exactly as it says in its name. It presents information in a graphic. They often convey facts, statistics and other findings in a colourful and vibrant way. These are a rising trend in the online community and become easier and easier to create every year. A few years ago, you would need to hire a graphic designer from Elance, Odesk or Fiverr to create one for you.

There are several advantages to making infographics which include gaining backlinks, easy social shares in your industry and more.

308. Video: A Full Experience
Video requires a lot more work than that of an article because you need so many tools to record the video, record your voice through a microphone and then all kinds of editing tools. However this investment is worth it, because with a video you have a **massive advantage** over the others in the rankings. By producing a video, you are guaranteed the first page at least, if not near the top. But this can only be achieved if your video is lengthy (more than five minutes) and has effective keyword research by including targeted keywords in the title and description.

When you've done your video, the best place to publish it is through YouTube. Google absolutely **loves** YouTube (they do own them after all). I've never ever seen a video that was on the second page. Creating a video on YouTube is one thing, but you can then embed it on your blog too and write an article surrounding it!

Have you ever noticed a YouTube video ranking at least third in the search results? It's those kind of videos that have been ranking well and creating videos are always a helpful ally to have in your back pocket.

309. Articles Should Be Primary, Infographics and Video Should Be Secondary

The type of content you create is completely up to you, but if I had to recommend a type, it would be article writing.

It is a lot less time consuming to write an article than design an infographic or record a video. However, mixing up articles with video and infographics is a proven tactic and boosts subscribers and customers. You choose whichever appeals to you more…not whichever is easier. I'm an article writer by heart, but I always like to create a few infographics!

Types of Articles

310. How To: The Art of Giving Instructions

This article teaches you how to do something in a step by step format from washing your car to studying the stars. There is no limit to what you can teach, and people will always encounter problems in everyday life. When they do, they will search Google with terms such as "how to rank well on Google" or "how to bake scones".

311. Numbered Lists: The Trending Favourite

The entire web and magazine world has caught onto this very valuable format of writing articles. I'm sure you're sick of these headlines, they're plastered all over social media and every blog you can think of. It's impossible to escape from them.

When you see a list headline, you automatically think "condensed, simple and bite-sized". In this busy and hurried world, people can skim lists quickly and get the main points rather than reading through a thesis.

Lists (or listicles, as social media folks call them) are super easy to write. All you have to do is get a topic or keyword, write ten tips/mistakes/questions about that and you're sorted! The most important part of a listicle is the title. You need to entice your readers with the title by turning the title into "click bait".

312. Ultimate Guides: Your Linkable Asset For The Future – Ultimate guides are an in-depth look at a certain topic. They can teach you how to do something, provide information or teach you everything there is to know about that topic. Ultimate guides are 3000-6000 word beasts which will gain traction, earn valuable links and become your linkable asset for the future.

You'll be spending at least two weeks, creating your ultimate guide. However, once it's published and you start prospecting for links – you'll get lots of backlinks from niche influencers. Since it's so useful, it will attract more and more people, who will share it/link to it, hence starting a vicious (but extremely satisfying) circle.

313. Curated Content: The Quick and Dirty Way To Get Direct Traffic
Curated content involves collecting links from around the web all circling on a particular topic and then pasting these links into your blog post. It could be a list of websites, tools, pages, resources, blogs, whatever. Examples include:
20 Interior Design Blogs Worth Watching In 2016
15 Articles That'll Teach You Everything About App Design
30+ SEO Tools That You Need To Use Right Now

Remember to sculpt the title around the content. Don't have something like, *"The Ultimate Guide To Keyword Research"* as your title, when the article has 50 links to keyword research articles from the web. Your title always needs to play to the reader's expectations. Failure to do so may result in a huge lack of trust and some very disgruntled readers.

314. Curate The Most Viral Images In Your Niche Into A Blog Post
These posts do extremely well and require little work on your part. All you need to do is find insanely amazing images, and then put them all together into a blog post. Slap a viral title onto the content, and you're good to go!

The question is, where do you find those insanely amazing images?

Look on Pinterest and Tumblr, and see what has gone viral in the last few months. Anything on Pinterest with more than 5000 repins is worth including. Make sure to locate the original photographer and ask them if you can use their image.

Be polite in your email, and don't feel intimated that you want to use their work. Most photographers are more than willing to give you their image, provided you give them attribution. It's a backlink for them, and more promotion.

Creating A Viral Piece of Content

315. Allocate A Time In The Week To Write
This part is often overlooked by most, simply because they think that writing is more of a hobby rather than a job. This mentality never works because people always attend to other tasks and leave their website hanging.

Right now, think of a suitable time when you will get to work on your website both on SEO and content. Make this time slot about two hours and write it into your diary, your fridge, your computer and your phone. Take a break between these two hours and refresh.
Stick to this plan as much as possible, because you will get a ton of work done each week.

316. Be In A Quite Writing Environment
Situations are different for many. You may prefer to write at home, in the library or on the train. Wherever it is, make sure that you have no distractions such as family, phones, internet and TV. These will become obstacles for you, and can really disrupt your work. Stay focused and work hard. You can check your emails, notifications and news after your two hours has completed.

317. Create An Outline Of Your Article

A lot of writers fear that they can't flesh out an article to 1500+ words. For every article you hope to write, prepare a quick outline of the sections before you begin. It doesn't have to be very intricate, just a quick look at what your article will cover.

318. Keep The Introduction Simple and Include Keywords

Start with a very brief introduction of what the article will cover. You can use your meta description as inspiration and flesh it out a little. The introduction doesn't have to be very elaborate, just keep it plain and simple. You can insert your targeted keyword(s) here too, which shows extra relevance to Google.

319. Use These Proven Introductions For Sales Copy

Want to turn readers into customers? Want to lure them into your products or services? Use a proven introduction for your sales pages.

This isn't an SEO tip as such, but is excellent for converting your readers into customers. It'll lead to a low bounce rate, increased conversions, more customers and higher page dwell time – which all in turn, help your SEO efforts.

Here are three proven introductions that you can use to turn a casual reader into a diehard customer.

1. **Bold Promise** – Promise your readers something bold and visionary. Make it look like you are re-inventing the wheel, changing society and revolutionizing a certain aspect of the world we live in today.

2. **Problem** – Address the problem, right in their face. Just slap it in front of them. See if they respond. More than likely, they'll have that problem and want to get rid of it. By doing this, at least they know that you can change their problem around forever.

3. **Story** – It was back in Third Grade. Graduation day. I looked around and standing there in front of me was…

That introduction pulled you in, right? Stories are an amazing way to grab attention instantly, and pull your customers heartstrings.

4. **Make A Shocking Statement** – Shock the reader by saying the unexpected. For example, "I'm a doctor, and I absolutely HATE diets. They make me reek." or "I got into MIT, one of the most prestigious universities in the world. The thing is, I hate studying."

320. Create Sub Headings For Extra Clarity
After your introduction, create sub-headings for each section you want to address. By splitting your article into lots of easy to digest sub-headings, readers can scan the sections they want to read more about. It also helps with your SEO because you can include some of your keyword phrases in these sub-headings.

321. Start Writing About Your Sub-Headings
Fill out your sub-headings by writing out all the information you have on that section. Make text engaging by making words **bold**, underlining, adding hyperlinks and *italics*.

322. Add One Personal Experience At Least
Add a **personal experience** here and there to spark some extra curiosity. It doesn't have to be a full biography, about 5-7 sentences is plenty. This just gives some extra credibility to what you have to say, and can help build a solid relationship between you and your reader who could potentially become a customer or subscriber.

323. Aim For 1500+ Words
By the time you finish your text, it should be about **1500+** words if it is going to rank well and attract backlinks from potential readers. People don't share the status quo – they share anything above that.

324. Basic Grammar Is An Essential

There are certain things that annoy readers and make you look stupid. One of them is being bad at grammar, "Their an awesome customer team.". Mixing up basic grammar rules such as "their, they're, there" looks awful and will turn everyone off.

Here is a list to some of the most common grammar mistakes people make. We all make mistakes, whether we are grammar geniuses or not. Often, when you get into the flow of creating a blog post – you may simply forget to put the right word in the right place. It happens.

Their, They're and There – *Their* is for possession. *They're* is short for "They are". *There* is for a location.

Apostrophe Use – Apostrophes are used in three ways.
- **Shortening words** – Whenever you shorten two words into one, use an apostrophe, "He's, They're, We've, That's, Could've."
- **Possession** – Use an apostrophe when indicating possession of an object or quality. "John's car runs so efficiently." If the name of the person ends with an 's', place the apostrophe at the end of the word.
- **Possessive Plural** – When using a possessive plural, put the apostrophe last. "The girls' dresses were lovely". The apostrophe positioned before the 's' would indicate that there was only one girl's dress, "The girl's dress."

Affect or Effect – *Affect* is to change or alter something. eg: "Black hat SEO can really affect your rankings"
Effect is the result or consequence of a change. "The effect of the Panda update was devastating, we were black hat SEOs."

Your or You're – *Your* is for owning something, "your scarf" whilst *you're* is short for "you are", "You're an awesome reader!".

Its or It's – *Its* is for owning something, "The cat drank its milk". *It's* is short for "it is", "It's a bright, sunny day!".

Accept or Except – *Accept* is to allow. *Except* is everything but that. "I will accept you into our school…except, you cannot enter the examination hall today."

Ensure or Insure – *Ensure* makes something definite, "Ensure that your website is accessible to crawlers". *Insure* is a financial or legal term, "Insure your car today!".

Then or Than – *Than* is used to compare two things, "Pink is better than blue." *Then* is used for everything else (point in time or after something). "It was great back then. Then, the storm came."

Could of, Would Of – You may think that the word "could've" is short for "could of" when it is actually *"could have"*. The same applies to would've and should've. They are short for *"would have and should have"*, not "would of or should of".

Principal or Principle – A *principle* is a fundamental law or truth that is accepted as true. A *principal* is an authority and a main thing. "The principal speaker made points on the principle of gravity."

Premier or Premiere – *Premier* is something of a higher quality. A *premiere* is the opening night of a film.

Farther or Further – *Farther* refers to physical distance, "How much farther until the beach?" *Further* refers to an extension of time or a degree. "The apprentice advanced further and became a master craftsman."

Complement or Compliment – A *complement* is to add to something. "The bracelet really complements the outfit." A *compliment* is a nice comment someone says about you.

I know this is an SEO book, and you're probably wondering why you're getting grammar lessons. But in reality, SEO is all about creating an amazing digital experience for the user and ranking highly for it. If your grammar is letting you down, you could get penalized for it from the next Google algorithm update.

325. Add A "Top Tips" Section
Here you can outline your best tips and tricks to succeed at whatever you're writing about. These tips are not your average bits of advice, but your finest and most useful. You'll see that most readers will enjoy reading your tips and can often quote them when sharing online. I happen to love reading *Top Tips* in articles because they are clear, super helpful and to the point.

326. Add A Summary
You can consolidate everything the article presented into bullet points. About five bullet points is sufficient and should reinstate everything the reader learned back into their mind. For an even better summary, try a "minfographic" (see below).

327. Include Some Quotes
You can provide little golden nuggets of wisdom from industry leaders and inspirational people here. No matter on what niches you're writing on, there are sure to be quotes available for you to use. Simply search "quotes on [your niche]" to find quotes on your niche.

328. Infographic Summary
You can also present a summary in infographic format. Here, you can condense the entire article into bullet points and present it as a "mini infographic" (I've called it a "minfographic"!). You can add icons here and there to illustrate your points. If you place social sharing buttons on the image, people are very likely to share it.

329. Create A Template That Will Help The Reader
You'd imagine that templates are only suitable for writing but you can create a template for anything such as art (templates for paintings, crochet or embroidery), gardening (templates for plots), DIY (templates for pieces of wood, stickers), writing anything at all (letters, emails, descriptions, book writing) music ("write your own songs") and so on. This is basically a "fill in the blanks to create your own" section that is extremely convenient for any reader. It lets them put your article into action and get a hands-on approach.

330. Include A Few Samples
To spark some inspiration, you can provide some sample ideas or examples. They don't have blanks like templates do but they present a fictional problem and then try to solve it through the sample. Eg: "Sally has had a bad experience at her local restaurant. She writes the following letter to the restaurant manager...". It helps readers apply their own problem to the situation and gives ideas on what to do next.

331. Throw In A Few Mini Case Studies
You can present real life examples of people who followed your information and got great results. Case studies are aimed primarily towards business/technology blogs but can work well with other niches when used creatively.

It is difficult to write a mini case study unless you are in contact with your readers but you can send subscribers an email saying you'd appreciate if anyone would like to be part of a case study if they found your results useful. You can create an article based on that case study and then for future articles, you can write a small paragraph on why your strategies worked for others. It's a great place to put a well-deserved internal link!

332. Include A "Warnings/Common Pitfalls" Section
Outlining common mistakes that people make is a lifesaver for everyone. It steers readers clear of failure and helps them to properly succeed. This establishes trust between you and the reader, and it shows a lot of experience and expertise in the area. Eg: *"Writing lots of short articles everyday does not equal one in-depth blog post once a week! Remember that it's about quality not quantity. Otherwise, you could end up in the doghouse."*

333. Add A "Your Toolbox" Section
Readers can learn of the tools that they need to start crafting. They don't have to be physical tools either, software and other web tools are great examples. You can present this at the beginning (however, a "What You'll Need" section is more relevant) or at the end (suited towards digital tools, rather than physical tools).

334. A Checklist Will Always Help
This is like a summary only it is aimed towards "how-to" articles that present the instructions in a step by step format. You can use a checklist for just about any "how-to" article no matter what niche it's in. You can present the checklist in text or image format, depending on what suits you more.

335. Videos Increase Engagement, So Add One
You can place these into your article to add an extra dimension. Multimedia completes the experience by including audio, moving imagery and an outside view of your topic. Multimedia also helps with SEO. Google love to see videos in your content so make sure to place at least one video in every article you write!
If there are no relevant videos to your topic, leave it. Video is more of a cherry on the cake, rather than the icing.

336. Add Images
Images are beautiful. They break up the monotony, add a sense of energy and really brighten up your page. People adore images, just as the success of Pinterest (photo sharing website) demonstrates today.

To stay in the content game, you need to add images and a lot of them. I've dedicated an entire chapter to choosing properly licensed (did you really think Google Images would solve it for you?) images that stun the world. As an extra, make sure to add a Made For Pinterest graphic (to get a lot of Pinterest traffic) and about five extra images.

337. Include A Text CTA's At The End
You can ask readers to share your content or comment by including one or two text CTA's (Call To Actions). Here are some examples.
"What's your opinion? Leave your comments below."
"What other methods to you like to use? Share it below."
"Share this article to let everyone else know!"
"Sharing makes the world go round. Contribute by liking this page."
"Make your voice heard! The best opinions in the comments below will be included in this article!"
"Any juicy knowledge you'd like to share? Mention it to me below and your comment could be shared on social media."

"Join the online trend. Share this page."
"Be a trendsetter and share this article with the world."
"Join 1390+ good-looking, intelligent people who shared this page." (hat tip: I got this idea from Buffer)

338. Keep Your Writing Easy To Read

It's very easy to get distracted and start writing long, complicated sentences. This can throw both people and search engines off course, as they'll find it hard to read (and crawl). Keep everything super easy to read, and make everything as "snappy" (quick n' snappy, as they say!) as possible.
Check if your writing is easy to read, by inputting the text into "Hemmingway Editor" (www.hemmingwayapp.com).

This super useful tool will tell you how easy/difficult it is to read your content, and will highlight sentences which are confusing and too long. It'll also point out common grammar mistakes too, which we could all use at some point or another!

339. Avoid Formatting Issues When Pasting From Word

If you are typing your blog post on Word and then paste it into your web editor, you could run into some formatting issues. TextCleanr (www.textcleanr.com) cleans your text and gets rid of any formatting that is unnecessary.

340. Change Microsoft Word Text To Clean HTML

If you don't have the option of pasting text, and can only write in HTML – you should convert it to HTML instead. Rather than coding it all out, it's so much easier to convert it to HTML. When using the tool, make sure to check the right boxes before converting to HTML. For example, some web editors use the <b> tag for bolding words rather than <strong>. (www.word2cleanhtml.com)

341. Remember Your On-Page SEO

Remember to implement on-page SEO for each and every article you write! By doing this, Google will find your page easy to read and super relevant. This will show very clearly what keywords you are targeting and more.

342. Disagree With Someone's Opinion, For More Traffic

This tactic works wonders.

Pick an opinion piece that annoys you and write a counter argument, in the shape of a a blog post. Mention the opinion piece that you're disagreeing with, and make points on why you disagree with them.

Remember, I said disagree. Not fight. Not troll. Not being a total b****. Just a friendly debate, done in a responsible way.

Avoid hugely controversial topics, and do not in any circumstance - start acting in a foolish manner. You'll only get a lot of hate, and could upset your customers.

For example, in the SEO sphere, Rand Fishkin made waves on the web when he disagreed with a blog post which praised Black Hat SEO and spoke of why White Hat SEOs are innocent little angels that are afraid to break the rules. Read it at http://bit.ly/1MzUq1W

Don't argue with the author or make points that aren't within the scope of the article. Keep any personal insults *out*, and leave them there.

Share your post with the author of the original opinion piece and ask them to share it on social media with a comment such as "Looks like someone has a bone to pick with me". It's a great way for them to show off their authority, and how they've actually caused a stir on the web.

343. Create Viral Content For Your Local Region

What's trending on Twitter, near you? Find out with www.trendsmap.com. By typing in your local city, you can find out what is trending and what resonates with the people in your local area.

If you have a local business, you might want to tap into this trend by creating content on it. Perhaps, an infographic wouldn't be worth the time or money for a local trend, but certainly an in-depth blog post or a series of memes/graphics would certainly do the trick. Share it with your followers on Twitter, with your family, you could even advertise locally with AdWords. If your content is wacky enough, you just might make the local radio or TV.

Repackaging Your Content

344. Add It To An eBook
You can't duplicate copies of blog posts on the web but you *can* duplicate your blog posts into an eBook. Whatever you publish on your blog can be placed into an eBook. Many bloggers have created books by simply pasting their past blog posts and formatting it in a way that makes it look like a professional book. You can do the same.

Publish through CreateSpace and Kindle Direct Publishing to make some extra cash. Or list your book for free and add a link to your website throughout the book, and it will get a lot of promotion.

345. Make A YouTube Video
If you have an aptitude for creating videos or podcasts, try making a video out of your article. Pick out your main points and add in some jokes. Upload your video once taped and add a link to your site in the description. Once the video is live on YouTube, make sure to embed the video on your site too, accompanied by a transcript.

346. Create An Infographic Out Of It
To Google, an image is an image, they can't read text (for duplication purposes). That means you can copy the contents of your article and create an infographic out of it. However, your fellow readers and subscribers may not be happy! That's why you should retitle the infographic and pick out the main points and statistics of your article, whilst mixing it up a little. Add some quotes too. You can publish this and get your well-earned backlinks!

347. Share Quotes And Statistics on Social Media

Pick out a quote, statistic or surprising fact from your article. Assemble it into a graphic and share it on social media. It is guaranteed to spread like wildfire! People much prefer to share and read articles that are shared in this way.

This will then create more opportunities for promotion and linkbuilding for you, if your quotes/stats reach niche influencers.

348. Repackage It Into A SlideShare

Pick out the main ideas of your article and paste them into a PowerPoint presentation. Add plenty of images and icons for visual appeal. Make the title of the SlideShare attention grabbing yet informative. Make sure that the thumbnail of the SlideShare is compelling by having an eye-catching image with the title imposed on it.

349. Quizzes Are Super Hot Right Now (No, Seriously!)

Research by Buzzsumo has found that out of the top ten pieces of content most shared online, eight of them were quizzes. Now that's something.

Something extraordinary.

Feed people's egos, they love it.
Create a quiz with no coding skills necessary at www.quizrevolution.com and embed the generated code on your site.
Make a short blog post alongside it, just to beef up your word count. The blog post could be something like "What Your Results Say About You" or "Joking Aside, Here's More Information About [Quiz Topic].

Quizzes are super-hot right now, but I haven't seen many bloggers actually taking advantage of them. Get on the bandwagon before anyone else. Your quiz has a very strong chance of going viral since online entertainment is a big hit on social media.

350. Replicate The Success of Content On Buzzsumo

Buzzsumo is a tool which shows you the most shared content in your niche. All you have to do is visit Buzzsumo at www.buzzsumo.com, type in your niche and see what articles are performing the best. Are they numbered lists? Do they challenge the status quo? Are they *different?* Make plenty of notes on what you see.

Try to replicate their success by titling your article in a similar fashion to theirs (I said *similar* not *copy*) and contain a unique twist that they haven't covered. If their content is mediocre, you can improve on it. Then, see who has been linking to their content and ask them if they could link to your article (which is so much better) instead.

Creating Predictably Viral Linkbait That'll Get Thousands of Links

Want to get more links? More traffic? Go viral? Here's a step by step guide. Whilst this is not a blueprint, it's certainly near enough to it.

351. Generate An Idea – This is the hardest part. Coming up with a viral idea is nearing that word called impossible. It certainly isn't as easy as "waking up in the middle of the night, with a billion dollar idea" (Larry Page, sound familiar?).
However, things like these often have a good shot of going viral:
- List Posts with a twist
- Infographics with a unique edge
- Comedy such as comics, memes on a particular niche – Ryan Gosling's SEO memes went viral, and they weren't exactly pieces of pure genius.

352. Test Your Idea
Take your best idea which you've been working on and send the following email to as many bloggers as you can think of. Ask them if they would like to share it, when you publish it in the future. If you get a positive response, you've got yourself a winner.
Hey [Name],

How are you? I really enjoyed reading your last post on [topic], it contained so much actionable strategies and advice. I've used a lot of your advice for my latest project.
I'm working on an infographic, which focuses on [what you're content is about]. Since you regularly share posts on this, and you're such an expert at [niche] – I'm sure your audience would love it.
The title is: [Title]
It's an infographic, so I was wondering if you could share it when it goes live? I would really appreciate it.
Let me know what you think,
[Your Name]

353. Craft Your Linkbait

Make your content stand out. Remember, great title, epic content, stunning visuals and all the other bells and whistles.

354. Find The Linkerati

Go to Buzzsumo and find the top influencers in your niche. Simply type your niche into the search bar, and select the "Top Influencers" tab.

You can also find a lot of niche influencers on Twitter. See who's being followed, and who you're following at the moment.

Bloggers and journalists in your niche are also great people to contact.

355. Ask The Linkerati To Share It

Send the perfect outreach email, as I have already covered in the Chapter 4. Again, be personalized, don't be blunt, send mid-week and keep it short.

356. Use All The Linkbuilding Techniques You Know

Get as many links as you possibly can to your piece of content. Promote. Promote. Promote.

The more quality links you can get to the linkbait, the more people will share and link to it in turn. Try and get it to go viral, because it has huge potential.

CHAPTER 10
Visual Content Marketing

The web is going visual. The following statistics show the true power of visuals:

- Blog posts with images receive **94% more views** than those without images
- Having at least one image in a post leads to more than **double the shares** on Facebook and Twitter [Study by OKDork]

It's time to take your fair share of the visual content marketing benefits.

Find Images To Use In Your Content and Website

357. Morguefile.

Here you have a wealth of superb, crystal clear images which look outstandingly good.

Morguefile (**www.morguefile.com**) covers everything from animals to beautiful landscapes to everyday objects from fruits to flowers, you name it. Many of the images are shot by professional photographers whilst others are shot by amateurs. You will get a mix of everything but it is well worth a try.

The images are free but you should always attribute back to the page giving the photographers name. You cannot modify the images. Remember to follow the image's licence at all times and sometimes you may need to contact the photographer.

358. Pixabay

My favourite photo site of all time is Pixabay. It's incredibly fast, powerful and offers a crisp interface. In terms of images, you will have hundreds of thousands of hi-res, stunning quality imagery that look as good as paid photos.

Best of all, every image on Pixabay is in the Public Domain! This means you can use it, modify it, do what you want with it all without attributing the photographer. So basically, it's yours for the taking! There aren't any licence terms to worry about. You will find beautiful images on their homepage updated every few days.

Pixabay cover almost everything you can think of. Their images are crystal clear and super sharp. Most of the images I use are from Pixabay simply because of their quality.
If there is one site you will give a try, it should be Pixabay. You won't be disappointed.

359. Freedigitalphotos.net
This website has thousands of images, graphics and diagrams that cover a wide range of topics. These images are mostly all shot by pro photographers but unfortunately, there is a downside. Some of the graphics have that cheesy "stock photo" feel. Whilst many of the images are fantastic, there are some which look like you downloaded them from a cheap stock site. Be aware of this and you won't have any trouble.

If you want to use one of the images, you can use the free version which has no watermarks, but you have to provide attribution. You cannot modify the images.
Some of the categories covered include:

- **People -** This website has a huge amount of photos with people, children and animals and includes images with businessmen and women, doctors, scientists, and many more roles.
- **Science, Health and Technology -** If you are a tech and science geek like me, you will find a good collection of science, medicine, health and technology images for your content.
- **Landscapes and Nature -** Depending on whether you are writing about animals, plants, gardens, landscapes or other forms of nature, you'll find a LOT of images in this category.
- **Food -** Like most sites, you will find a good amount of food and drink photos here, just watch out for anything cheesy (pun intended) because there are a few.

- **Clipart** – Freedigitalphotos.net have a fair advantage with clipart. They contain the most clipart I've ever seen covering literally everything.
- **Business** - You will find an extensive range of images in many subcategories including agriculture, finance, charts, business people, offices, energy, and many more.

360. Unsplash

In terms of photo quality, this is the best you can get. The images that you'll find on this site look like priceless images because of their size, quality and awesomeness.

All images were shot by professional photographers and were released into the Public Domain. This means you can use and modify them without attribution. Every ten days, ten new images will be released. You might even get some inspiration from them!

361. Little Visuals

This Tumblr blog works similarly to Unsplash. You get 7 new hi-res images every 7 days. These images are submitted by professional photographers and are released into the Public Domain. Simply epic images.

362. Wikimedia Commons

Whilst painfully organized, do a search on www.commons.wikimedia.org and you should find plenty of images on whatever you want. This puts function over form. You will find images of pretty much everything. All images used in Wikipedia articles are from Wikimedia Commons, so you can use those images too.

Just keep in mind that every image has a different license. One image may need attribution whilst another might be in the Public Domain. You will find the license terms written in plain English underneath the image. Adhere to the license terms carefully.

Creating A Made-For-Pinterest Graphic

363. Join The MFP Revolution
Going viral is easy. You just need to do it right. By creating an MFP graphic, you can generate thousands of views from Pinterest and really appeal to niche influencers. All you have to do is follow the steps below. People these days love sharing images with text imposed on them. These are MFP graphics (see an example below).

364. Use Canva To Create MFP Images
Canva is a free design tool which allows you to edit images and create stunning designs with text, icons, backgrounds, frames and so much more. Log onto www.canva.com and click on the design you'd like to create. I would recommend either a social media graphic, presentation graphic or blog post graphic for optimum sizes.

The thing that sets Canva apart in the crowded design world is the super-professional templates available. You select what kind of design you want to create such as a blog post image, a Facebook header, a business card or an advertisement among many others. You can modify these templates by adding images, background, icons and text.
There are tens of templates that appeal to a variety of categories. Whatever niche you are in, there will most definitely be a style that you'll like!

After that, add text to the image so that the title is clearly visible on the image. Here is an example of a fantastic MFP image:

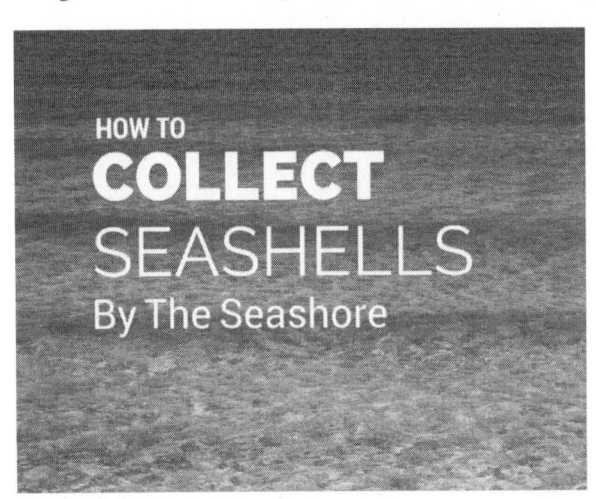

HOW TO
COLLECT
SEASHELLS
By The Seashore

You can also add icons and patterns to your image too, so use them if you feel the need.

365. Keep Text On Image To A Minimum
Make sure to include the title of your article as the only text in the design! Don't clog up the design with unnecessary text. Keep the main title plain and simple. You don't have to stick to the exact title either, you can always switch it around.

For example, instead of saying "20 SEO Tricks That Will Increase Your Rankings Today", you could say "Increase Your Google Rankings - 20 SEO Tricks". Just keep the main essence of the title in the front and the rest can follow.

366. Make It POP At A Small Size
Make sure the title is bold and can be easily read from a credit card size (average Pinterest image size). Make the text stand out by contrasting dark on white or vice versa. It's got to be vivid and remind you of a soda can. In short, make it pop.

367. Make The Image Flow
Keep the design style similar to the subject you are presenting. The best way to tie the whole design together is to use colour schemes, typography and imagery which all resonate with one another. For example, a modern and thin font contrasts well with a serene, blue sea. It wouldn't look as good in a rock concert! Similarly, a jagged, rocky font wouldn't work on an image with cupcakes!

368. Icons Are Hot Right Now
Place an icon above a heading to pack an extra punch. Canva have thousands of icons and drawings for you to choose from. Even one icon will really emphasise what your image is about, all in a matter of seconds!

… CHAPTER 10: VISUAL CONTENT MARKETING

Infographics

369. Piktochart.com
Probably the cutest, most useful and easiest infographic tool out there. With ready to use templates, over 4000 icons, images and a beautiful interface, you'll be on your way to steal-worthy infographics. Creating a professional infographic is possible in minutes. All you need to do is sign up for a free account, select a template and write in your own facts and stats!

370. Easel.ly
With tons of templates (more than piktochart.com), you can create professional infographics in a matter of moments. You don't need to sign up for an account with easel.ly and everything is free. More than 700,000 infographics have been created on easel.ly, showing just how trendy infographics are today.

371. Venngage.com
This is another free tool which allows you to create dozens of beautiful infographics, all for free. There are of course, premium options but the main infographic templates are for free.

372. Canva.com
This is probably the best graphic design tool that you can use, but I must say that it's functionalities for infographics are limited since they don't have infographic templates you can use for free.
However, they have literally thousands of icons, graphs, charts, diagrams, text holders and other "infographic elements" that you can use to create your infographics.
If you want to create your infographic from scratch and want some amazing placeholders and icons to add to your infographic, Canva is probably the best option for you.

373. Get Free Icons
If you find that you are limited on icons for your infographics, you can find millions of icons on the following websites.
- **The Noun Project** – Get thousands of icons and icons of common nouns, through this website. Almost anything you can think of has become an icon in this innovative project. Most of the icons are in the Public Domain whilst others require attribution. (www.thenounproject.com)

- **Icomoon.io** – Get icons of practically anything you want. Adjust the icons by size, colour and file type. Simply choose the icons you want and download as an icon pack. The icons are all free, but for specific packs you need to pay.
- **Iconfinder.com** – Get free icons and vectors on this site. Many of the icons are in full colour giving you even more reason to get creative.

374. Include These Elements In Your Infographics

Every infographic needs to include the following elements, no matter what.

- **Facts** – Make statements. Give an introduction. Keep facts short but incredibly powerful.
- **Statistics** – Throw in a few statistics too which are sure to shock your audience. Try and use a variety of data visualization techniques such as pie charts, bar charts, line plots, image representations and even, sentences. The more creative your statistics are displayed, the more shares your infographic will get. Easy as that. Think outside the box.
- **Quotes** – A simple but inspirational quote from a thought leader can really turn your infographic from a piece of information to an actionable, inspiring one. And when you inspire others, that's when the shares come.
- **Graphs** – Make sure to portray your statistics and raw data in a visual format using graphs and charts. The more creative you get with your graphs, the better.

375. Be Unexpected, Surprise Them

The more you surprise the reader, the more likely they are going to share your infographic. The best way to surprise them is with shocking statistics and facts.

For example, did you know that out of 250 babies born, a whopping 113 are born into poverty – every minute?

Or that 120,673 pounds of edible food is thrown away in the US, every sixty seconds?

Shocking stats, right?

Those facts appeared on an infographic entitled "20 Things That Happen Every Minute", by Online Education. The statistics were shocking and I was genuinely impressed by both the content and the graphic design of the infographic. That infographic became super famous and went more than just viral, it got on TV. Reporters cited from it, journalists wrote about the infographic and everyone on social media were mentioning the statistics from it. You can check it out at: www.onlineeducation.net/every_minute All because of twenty statistics which surprised the world.

376. Titles You Can Use For Your Infographic – Here are some catchy and viral titles you can use for your infographic. Even if you don't know what topics to cover in your infographic – take a read through the titles and change them for your own infographic.

Geek Versus Nerd [Infographic]
A Brief History of The Internet In Graphics
The 100 Top Selling [Books/Songs/Products Related To Your Niche] of All Time
20 Shocking Things That Happen Every Hour
The Visual Guide To Goal Setting (That Actually Works)
The 20 [Discoveries/Innovations/Trends] That Changed The World In [2015/Last Decade/Last Century]

377. Linkbuild With Your Infographic
We aren't creating infographics for art, you know! The reason why you're going to the effort of creating an infographic is to use it's incredible linkbuilding potential. Make sure to tap into all that potential link juice with your infographic! One infographic can really get your website ranking higher on Google for the keywords you want, so keep that in mind.

378. Google Public Data Is Great For Statistics
Need some statistics for your infographic? This interesting project from Google displays information from public databases allowing you to do some research. Get all kinds of facts, figures and statistics here. It's perfect for finding some stats for your next article or infographic.

379. Prospect Google For Statistics
If you're looking for statistics in your niche, and can't seem to find them on any open data websites, just prospect Google for statistics. Enter the following search strings:

"[your niche] statistics"
"[your niche] research"
"[your niche] data"

You'll find hundreds of articles and blog post which either contain third party research or research conducted by themselves. Make sure to keep a track record of where you get your statistics from, as you'll need to provide attribution in your infographic!

380. Other Open Data Websites
Sometimes, you'll find the perfect set of data that you need on these websites.
www.thedatahub.org
www.data.gov
www.datamarket.com
www.census.gov
www.datacatalogs.org
www.data360.org
www.freebase.com

A lot of the data hasn't been digged up and used yet, so get working that data into your infographic!

381. Get Quotes For Your Infographic
Adding in quotes really strengthen your infographic from people that we just can't get enough of. When you make a fact or statement, throw in a quote to back up your argument. Getting quotes is easy, simply take a visit to QuoteBrain or input these search strings to Google. Pick the most inspiring, world changing, breathtaking quotes you've ever seen and place them in your infographic. Drama wins shares.
"[your niche] quotes"
"[your niche] nuggets of wisdom"

CHAPTER 10: VISUAL CONTENT MARKETING

382. Cite Your Sources At The End
It mightn't look the most glamorous but when you cite the sources of the statistics and research in your infographic at the end, you build trust with the reader, show that your statistics are true and after all, it's only fair.

383. Add Your Website Logo At The End
Just in case your infographic goes viral or gets copied, you need to show who created the infographic in the first place. By adding your website or company logo at the end, you show who created that infographic in the first place.

Place your logo in the bottom right corner but don't place it at the start of the infographic. Then, it just looks like you're hogging the limelight. And no one likes that.

No one.

384. No Promotion In Your Infographic
Don't under any circumstances, start promoting your company in the middle of the infographic or start rambling on about your products or services.

Something like this isn't acceptable either, *"Over 50% of backlinks that websites receive are spam links, according to research. The only way to get out of this SEO trap is to purchase our link checker which checks your backlinks so that you can see if any spam sites are still linking to you."*

The only promotion you can add into your infographic is your website logo at the end. But, nothing more than that.

385. Size Matters
Keep your width at a recommended level of 600 pixels. Since some users may have a slow internet connection, the maximum size of your infographic should be 1.5MB. Length wise, keep your infographic at a maximum length of 7500-8000 pixels. Whilst infographics are supposed to be lengthy and big, going over certain limits means that you start to lose potential readers.

386. Get Your Infographics Outsourced
If you feel that you're design skills aren't up to par, or just feel like giving the task to someone else, you can outsource your infographics at a small cost.

Try Fiverr, Odesk, Elance for designers that'll make you an infographic at a cheap price.

Make sure not to pay more than $100 for your infographic because you can get high quality infographics for a lot cheaper and there's no need to go paying any more than $100 for an infographic. Some companies can charge up to $500 for an infographic, so as you can see – the price varies wildly!

387. Include A Lot of White Space

You'd be surprised at how few bloggers forget to include white space. They pile statistics, charts and graphs on top of each other, leading to nothing but a stewing hot mess. Make sure your infographic has enough white space which allows the viewer to breathe a little.

388. Do A "Versus" Infographic

These infographics are wildly popular at the moment and will continue to be popular in the future. Pick two contrasting things or themes in your niche and compare them.

Themes like people (geeks, hipsters), hobbies (electric guitar, acoustic guitar) and objects (sugar, sweeteners) can easily be incorporated into your infographic.

Examples: "Geek Versus Nerd"
"Web Design Versus Web Development: What's The Difference?"
"iOS Versus Android: The Stats"

389. Pay For Stumbles, on StumbleUpon – It costs about $0.10 for a stumble (click to your website) on StumbleUpon.

Users of SU love infographics and especially ones with a shocking surprise or some badass statistics. If you want to start going on the road to viral, one of the best ways to get your infographic into the public is with paid advertising on StumbleUpon.

It's cheap, targeted towards an infographic savvy audience and will start clocking up immediate interest to your infographic.

390. Promote, Promote , Promote (Times A Million)

Use all the linkbuilding strategies I've talked about in the Chapter 4. If you've done some of the research yourself and found some startling, shocking or unsettling statistics, you deserve to make a press release out of it. Submit your press release to several journalists and press release distribution sites.

Make sure that your infographic can be embedded. Ask influencers to share your infographic. Submit it to infographic directories. Pay for StumbleUpon traffic.

Once your infographic is published, you need to get it out there. It has huge potential, and a good chance of going viral. That's why you need to promote it and send out emails to people like a broken fire main.

Other Images You Should Create

391. Quote Images
Create some quotes using Canva. They will go viral on Pinterest, Twitter and even, Instagram. As the saying goes, "You're only as deep as your last Instaquote."

You can also create some "quote articles" which will give you extra social media traffic. Other tools to create quotes include Quozio or Recite. The creativity of these tools are limited, but are faster than Canva.

392. Screenshotted, Annotated Images
If you want to take any snapshots of your computer or annotate images, download Skitch at www.evernote.skitch.com. This allows you to annotate your images using text, pixilation (hiding emails or passwords), boxes, stamps or arrows all in a variety of colours. If you are doing a tutorial of any kind, just upload your image (or take a screenshot) and start annotating! It will greatly help your reader to follow instructions.

393. Charts
When displaying data of any kind, create charts using www.infogr.am. This nifty tool works similar to graphs on Excel but gives you more functionality. A must have for any chart reliant niche.

394. Images In Tech
Ever seen a picture with a website inside a smartphone, tablet or desktop? You can do the same. Simply head over to www.placeit.com and upload your website image. Drag the image into the piece of technology and download! You can use this for all your marketing, advertising and even blog posts.

395. Wordle
Create striking word clouds with this tool. Simply input your words and get a generated cloud from those words. You can then change colours and fonts.

396. Patterns
You can add patterns to your website background, blog posts or even MFP images. Find amazingly vibrant pattern designs at www.thepatternlibrary.com. Patterns include fruit, flowers, design tools, alchemy and magic, subway lines, optical illusions and many more. You have got to see them. Use them for any kind of visuals you're thinking of creating from web headers to MFP graphics.

397. Memes
Got some crazy jokes you want to share? Memes are comedy for the web, and there's no reason why you shouldn't create a few. Social media love these and one meme is enough to give you considerable social media traffic. Make your own at www.mememaker.net/create or www.imgflip.com/memegenerator. It only takes a few seconds to make one, and could really get your brand out there. You're subscribers and customers all love a chuckle too.

While I'm on the topic of memes, my favourite meme series of all time is probably Ryan Gosling's SEO memes. Cheesy but super funny and incredibly satisfying when you actually understand them. After you've read this book, and have become an SEO expert – check them out and see if you "get" the jokes. If you do, congrats! You are officially an SEO nerd.

CHAPTER 11
Incredible Tips From The SEO Experts

I asked the following SEO experts and bloggers what their number one tip was for both content marketing and SEO. Here are their answers. You'll find a lot of varied answers, some similar and some wildly different.

Peter Doman, Vancouver SEO Company (www.vancouver-seo-company.com)

398. Be consistent, and have a passion for what you do

The number one marketing tip that you need to do for SEO is be consistent. Make time to do the same processes so that you can measure the results of the work that you are doing. There is no silver bullet that fixes everything. It takes time and consistency to get the results that you want.

The number one content marketing tip is to be authentic, congruent and original in all the materials that you write. Write with a passion that shines through for the chosen field that you work in. Show people that you care about the topic. This translates to people wanting to deal with you because of your magnetism and boldness in having passion about what you do.

The best strategy to gaining more traffic is to combine organic marketing with face to face marketing and being able to talk to people about what you do. This then combines with the option of paying for clicks on Facebook, Google, Linkedin, Youtube and Pinterest.

Ron Johnson, CyberOptik (Digital Marketing Agency, Chicago) (www.cyberoptik.net)

399. Create content that matches your business

Provide useful content on your website that someone would find value in. For example, if you install ponds, you should write a group of articles/resources related to ponds. For example, "The different types of ponds", "The general costs that go into installing a pond", "Ongoing maintenance costs for a pond", "How to maintain your own pond", and even "How to build your own pond". Articles like this are going to be beneficial for SEO because people are actually going to want to read this content. It's also going to help brand you as a pond expert and increase your credibility once someone reaches out to you.

Orun Bhuiyan, SEOcial (Search Marketing Agency, New York and Vancouver) (www.seocial.com)

400. Links are the currency of search engines, continue to build them.

There's a lot of nonsense out there surrounding SEO. Everyone is always releasing information, Google publicly announces their advice and updates, etc.

There's so much information and misinformation that it's easy spend all of your time absorbing it and none of your time attaining results. This is deliberate. Search engines don't want to be manipulated so they dilute the information that's truly useful with inconsequential data.

My one tip would be to build links and don't get distracted. Links are the currency of search engines and they're the only element of your campaign that must be executed consistently. Everything else is secondary.

Liz Mazzei, Marketing Consultant (www.lizmazzei.com)

401. Optimize your URLs, create content that is of value and reach out to others outside your circle

What is your number one SEO tip?
Make sure your URL's are optimized! Think about how, which keyword phrases you are targeting and how the content on your website will be organized before finalizing your URL structure. So many of my clients come to me with sites that have URLs with just numbers and long strings of useless information asking me how to optimize their site. Start by having your URLs match the keyword phrases you are targeting and the title of the page.

What is your number one content marketing tip?
Provide useful information that will position yourself as an expert in your community. Create and share information that will be of value and then distribute that information on appropriate channels.

What is your best strategy to gaining more traffic?
Don't forget to create a dialog with your partners, complimentary service providers, industry organizations. These organizations may not be your primary customers but they have access to a completely different audience of your target customers. Reach more people by going outside of your normal circle.

Takeshi Young, SEO Manager at Optimizely (www.optimizely.com)

402. Be interesting

What is your number one SEO tip?
Be interesting. Although Google looks at hundreds of factors when ranking websites, links are still the most important one, and one of the best ways to attract links is to be interesting. Either have an interesting product, create interesting content, or do something that is interesting or newsworthy. If you are interesting it makes link building as simple as reaching out to people who would be interested in you and letting your content spread organically through social media.

What is your number one content marketing tip?
Spend as much time researching and promoting content as you do actually creating it. Too many marketers out there create tons of content without doing their research to see what will be successful, and they don't promote the content enough once it's created. Research and promotion are key to content marketing success.

What is your best strategy to gaining more traffic?
Create relevant content for topics that people are searching for. That's the simplest way to gain more organic traffic coming to your site.

Stephen Nuttall, Online Marketing Consultant (www.stephenmnuttall.com)

403. Optimize your site for people, not search engines.

Search engines were created for people, not for websites or webmasters, and they are getting better and better at refining the way they provide people with relevant information. While there are still some kinks in the system, they have come a long way from the days of being able to manipulate an algorithm and spam your way to the top.

You can't just do one piece of the puzzle anymore and succeed, it's about having a cohesive strategy for all aspects. If you're optimizing for search engines, there's a good chance there will eventually be an algorithm change that will nullify those strategies.

Optimize for people and create engaging content with the intention of answering questions and a great user experience. Doing this will translate to success in the search engines.

Alex Bungener, Local SEO Expert (www.localsearchoptimizationservices.com)

404. Have a mobile website and write content for humans, not bots

Most important I think is having a mobile optimized website via a responsive website WITH phone and map buttons (if a business).

Write content that targets a keyword phrase in an educational or informative, interesting or entertaining way. Write for humans not bots. I think within a couple of years Google's "artificial intelligence" will be able to know the keyword phrases that best fit the content without any of those keyword phrases existing in the content.

Social media is the best way to drive traffic to your site or blog post quickly. SEO is best for traffic over the long term.

Brad Titus, SEO Analyst (www.bltitus.com)

405. Build great content and get people to talk about it

I've been doing SEO for about six years, and the industry has changed tremendously in that time because of how much Google has changed their algorithms and their rules. Any SEO you talk to is going to tell you about Penguin and Panda and the new landscape of SEO, but the fact remains that the best type of organic marketing is what it always has been - building great content and getting people to talk about it.

Google has gotten increasingly better at finding people who are trying to game the system and cheat to improve their rankings, embracing grey hat or black hat strategies. A successful organic marketing strategy is easy to explain, but challenging to execute (because it requires intentional, consistent effort and patience to see it work) - figure out who your audience is, create the content that both you and your audience finds interesting, and make it easy for your audience to share it.

All of the other metrics of good marketing - worrying about bounce rate and page views and time on site and site architecture and headers and H1 tags and meta tags and descriptions and everything else - all of this goes back to making sure your content is good and that you've made it easy for your content to be shared.

Mary Long, Digital Media Ghost (www.digitalmediaghost.com)

406. Link to your own pages in your blog posts

What is your number one SEO tip?
Write posts for your website with a plan for linking back to other posts (on your website). People are too quick to link away to other sites and don't link to their own pages as often as they should.

What is your number one content marketing tip?
Curating content is great, but it needs to be focused, not random - or your results will be random too. What does systematic content curation look like? Make sites you plan to share from a part of your content marketing plan - research them and share purposefully, focused around themes that relate to the content you're currently writing. Putting order to the chaos will help you better understand what your audience loves/hates and hone your content (and curation) moving forward.

What is your best strategy to gaining more traffic?
Most people misunderstand content marketing and spend too much time on the "content" side and not nearly enough on promotion. Developing a significant digital footprint should be part of any good content marketing

plan. That doesn't mean having a bazillion followers, it means interacting and networking with your target audience and consistently expanding your reach. As part of that, you should share connections' content as freely as your own and view competitors as potential collaborators.

Michael Bergen, Content Marketing Manager at Riverbed Marketing (www.riverbedmarketing.com)

407. Content leads to more customers

What is your number one SEO tip?
Avoid cheaping out on "cookie cutter" SEO packages and tools that offer a specific amount of links, blog posts, or articles published. The money you save on cutting corners, will be lost in time and money spent correcting the problems caused by the inexperienced.

What is your number one content marketing tip?
Don't create content you think is good, create content your audience appreciates. Have common questions, objections, or customer feedback that comes back regularly? These topics deserve a permanent place on your website!

Educate your visitors with the answers to the questions they seek. This builds trust and nurtures the buying experience.

What is your best strategy to gaining more traffic?
Target your content around educating and solving industry relevant questions or problems your customers face. Ensuring you take due diligence in having the information that is sought after is key to improving traffic.

Half the battle is getting them to the website, but without substance to hold the audience on the site, there is no traffic to improve.

Sheryl Boddie, CEO of Marketing Media Management (www.managemmm.com)

408. Start with the end in mind

What is your number one SEO tip?
Whether your online goal is to sell product(s),
book appointments or simply expand awareness of your brand, decide what you will measure, then craft your SEO strategy around it.

For example: If your goal is to gather email addresses for a new Farmer's Market opening in Seattle, Washington so you can build a list for future marketing, then your end goal might be to measure the number of Email Subscription Submissions. Knowing that is the goal trigger, now decide the goal funnel path, your target demo and what SEO tactics you will need to use within the funnel.

We would most likely complete a Tapestry Profile to identify the psychographics of our target market and then perform keyword research. Then ask yourself, what website changes will we need? How much SEO Real Estate currently exists on our website and blog for this campaign and what will we need to create? What keywords from our research are most likely to attract people to our pages and posts? What high value external backlinking opportunities exist for this campaign? What opportunities to place article content or online Press Releases for our campaign exist?

Once you have those questions answered, it's time to implement!

Ongoing, you will want to consistently measure your website SEO activity and outcomes against your goals. What changes need to be made? Take your time in creating the strategy, but quick to make changes based on the metrics and goal conversions.

What is your number one content marketing tip?
Know your target demographic and understand that you MUST develop a strategy for your content that helps you reach people where THEY are and not where YOU THINK they are. Just placing your content on one channel won't get it seen.

What is your best strategy to gaining more traffic?
Understand that SEO, Social Media and Content Marketing are all connected and craft your online marketing strategy that way. The amount of traffic you gain is dependent on how completely you use all of these activities and tactics within your online marketing sales funnel to attract your ideal target market.

Shelley Hunter, Content Manager for GiftCards.com

409. Just Write.

When I first started blogging, I didn't know anything about SEO. When my website got acquired by a larger company, an in-house SEO expert began teaching me the basic principles of "writing for robots." I did my own research as well. The more I followed the advice I received, the more search traffic my blog posts netted. However, I also found the writing to be a little mechanical—forcing keywords where I would have preferred to say something different, overthinking headers and worrying about word counts.

Overtime, however, I got comfortable enough with the rules that I didn't have to think so much about them and discovered that good content would be successful even if I didn't follow every single tip.

So my SEO advice is this: after reading all the tips on SEO and listening to all the experts, just write. Write good content that answers the questions people are asking. Stay on topic and say what needs to be said. When your post is done, you can go back and switch a few words or shift header tags around as needed to strengthen the SEO value.

But don't get so locked into the rules that you forget to be a writer.

Doug Motel, Author of "101 Marketing Tips For Tourism" (www.siteoptimized.com)

410. Videos can really increase your traffic, and get customers from social media

What is your number one SEO tip?
Forget about the search engines and pretend you are creating a website that is a hub of information related to your goods or services. The result is that you will naturally be creating keyword rich content and people will naturally be linking to you.

What is your number one content marketing tip?
Videos. Create videos, even videos that are stills with narration.

Why?

Because you can re-purpose a video for all of your social media platforms and you can transcribe the audio and turn it into rich text content. A video can hit a flock of birds with one stone.

What is your best strategy to gaining more traffic?
Videos again. Create a video that is either super funny, super informative or super sexy and get it onto social bookmarking sites. It can go to places you had never even imagined...

Scott Benson, Founder of Benson SEO and Former Lead SEO for Vocus, PRWeb and HARO (www.bensonseo.com)

411. Create pain point marketing content

Quite simply, pain point marketing content revolves around answering your target market's questions (pain points) with content before they ever arrive at your site.

There's a Forrester study stating 93% of all online experiences start with a search engine. Each phrase people enter on search engines is a query, a question that needs answering. Creating content to address those questions is a great content marketing win for any business, especially smaller companies that can't compete with larger brands in the search listings for competitive terms.

Pain point marketing content doesn't always generate the highest volume of traffic, but it attracts customers when they are searching for help. You can often see this in the length of the queries, as they tend to be longer and much more specific. You ensure targeted traffic to your site, and traffic that is primed to convert.

Research is key to successful pain point marketing. If you can find a few willing existing customers, you'll be able to ask them directly, "what problems can this website help you solve?" Additional information can be found in on-site search queries – these are the terms site visitors enter on your website search form. Potential customers are telling you exactly what they need or can't find easily on your site.

Michelle Ruiz, Insite Creative (www.insitelongisland.com)

412. Choose keywords with slightly less searches, but significantly less competition

Do your research. Don't decide automatically that you want to rank for Keyword A that gets 20,000 searches a month, because it may turn out that you have 40,000 competitors. Instead, choose keywords that may get slightly less searches, but have significantly less competition. You may be able to rank for those much more easily, and get the combined results comparable to if you had ranked for your original favorite.

James Blews, Online Marketing and SEO Consultant (www.jamesblews.com)

413. Reach out to influencers with killer content

What is your number one SEO tip?
SEO is a method, not an action, as some newer users of SEO will find out. As such, patience is your biggest strength, and my biggest tip; have patience. Rankings, when done for the long-term, with quality in mind, will take time, but will yield the most impact in organic search traffic. Whether Google has performed an update and a brand's rankings are dropping, or some competition that is 'churn-and-burn' with their content and their links which have bumped your website...stay calm and be patient.

What is your number one content marketing tip?
The best content marketing tip I can provide is to find the answers, not just information. As consumers are using digital means for everything, from blind dates to buying groceries, content should follow suit; and find the answers to anything and everything a user would want. Not only will content creators and website owners find more traffic by becoming an answer, they will find a community by becoming THE answer.

What is your best strategy to gaining more traffic?
One of the best strategies for generating quality traffic is to mix video marketing with paid for advertising (Facebook Ads and Google AdWords). With that said, the direct traffic isn't what I'm looking for. I'm looking for opt-ins and email signups for a 'cheat sheet' of social media info or a checklist for SEO or local SEO or an upcoming webinar or something of value, but for free. That email is worth a future sale later on, and so, you should be giving time to landing page design, traffic and lead generation and copywriting skills, as much as writing articles.

The other strategy is using influencers and outreach for traffic. This approach allows you to create killer content (in any media form), and then to directly content influencers, on an industry and regional level, to get your brand name known.

Sometimes this involves creating content that includes them (expert list, ask for a quote on a subject, etc). Other times, it's about you helping to meet the needs and questions of their viewership and community. Either way, it a safe, impactful and very beneficial type of relationship to start building.

Dave Davies, CEO of Beanstalk Internet Marketing (www.beanstalkim.com)

414. Write two different types of copy: copy that will convert your visitors, and copy that will attract links

What is your number one SEO tip?
Link building is a PR exercise. Links are what tells the engine your content is more equal than others. Focusing your link energies on links that are geared to driving traffic will ensure that the links you build are more likely to hold weight.

What is your number one content marketing tip?
Write two different types of copy, the content to convert your visitors and the content to attract the links, social signals and to answer questions.
People aren't generally going to share your services page but they will share a page of metrics on your industry.

What is your best strategy to gaining more traffic?
Rank highly. ;)

Dan Smith, SEO Specialist at Leighton Inc (www.leighton.com)

415. Optimise for the user, not the search engine

SEO is no longer about optimising your website for the search engines - it's about optimising your entire digital presence for the user, ensuring they can gain access to the content they're looking for as quickly, as easily and as effectively as they can. From your social media activity through to your on-site experience, tailor it all to the user and you'll see not just increased organic traffic, but increased conversions.

Kate Proykova, Managing Director of Hop Online (www.hop-online.com)

416. Write content that has niche keywords and focuses on certain buyer personas

What is your number one SEO tip?
Try to find niche keywords and build your strategy around them. Niche keywords are keywords with decent search volume and low competition (e.g. the sites that rank on page 1 in Google for that search term have low Page Rank / Domain Authority).

What is your number one content marketing tip?
Know your buyer persona(s) and combine the content you create for them with keyword optimization. This way you (1) target your buyers with the content they need and (2) build the ground for ranking organically and gaining free traffic with the keywords you target.

What is your best strategy to gaining more traffic?
Writing keyword optimized content is the best strategy for any online business. It is a long-term approach, but its effect lasts long as well.

CHAPTER 11: INCREDIBLE TIPS FROM THE SEO EXPERTS

Collin Jarman, Jr. Digital Analyst at COCG (www.cocg.co)

417. Be specific, and the right customers will come

There are lots of SEO tips that come to mind, though if I had to pick one, it would be to "find your niche." Figure out what makes you unique. What's a problem your business can solve that few others can? What's an area you're knowledgeable in that could help others out?

To illustrate with an example: it's one thing to sell clothes at your store. It's a step up to sell "custom & special order clothes." It's even better to sell "custom & special order clothes at Brier Creek, in Raleigh, NC."

Be specific about what you have to offer. Whether you're selling a specialized product that serves a niche group of consumers, or you're blogging about an obscure topic that will be helpful to people with a very specific problem, you need to describe your services in a way that makes you a clear fit for what your target audience is searching for. Be specific about your product and where you are geographically, if it applies.

If you do this correctly, the traffic will come. Depending on your niche it may be a lot or a little, but in most cases, quality of traffic trumps quantity. Set up goals so you know if visitors are buying from you. If not, consider changing your messaging. If they are, then you know you've properly appealed to your niche market. Now that you know your market, you can expand to paid search ads, banner ads, social media, etc to grow your audience.

Kathryn Bisson, Technology Seed (www.tseed.com)

418. Follow the latest trends, and Google algorithm changes

The one tip that I would provide any business is to do your research and create compelling content. As new technologies and social channels are released, individuals will learn new engagement strategies and change business interactions. With all these changes, it is essential, as a digital marketer and SEO strategist, to be knowledgeable about the trends so when you do create compelling content it is ranked and it reaches your audience. Not only do you need to follow audience trends, but you need to remain up-to-date on Google algorithm changes as well.

Neal Fondren, Senior Vice President for Digital Strategies and Insights at Intermark Group (www.intermarkgroup.com)

419. Focus on content, and you'll bring the traffic to your site

Search engines are designed to provide users with the most relevant information based upon a search query. The last thing a search engine wants to do is connect a user to information that is irrelevant. In order to do that, search engines have begun to focus heavily on content and far less on keywords.

The best tip I can provide is to encourage website operators to focus on two aspects of their content:

1. Think in terms of content themes. A website cannot be all things to all people. Every site has subjects they own. I like to call them content pillars. These are subjects that are a business or organization's sweet spots. Content needs to be organized within a structure that provides a search engine's spiders (and your Web visitors) with a clear message: this is what we do. When a site is organized in pillars of content, structuring the URL becomes natural and follows the content pillar. Find your pillars and build

content around them.

2. Don't use content to game the system. Search engines like Google have publically stated that they will be discounting sites an use content as means to stuff keywords into content in the hopes of rising in organic search listings. Don't be tempted. Take an honest and forthright approach to content development.

In developing content, bear in mind that you aren't looking for all the users, but rather the right users. Employing a content strategy that is full of information relevant to the user is the way to bring the right traffic to your site.

Marian Rothschild, (www.marianrothschild.com), Author of "Look Good Now and Always"

420. Write for other websites, and you'll get lots of exposure

Get as many outside links coming in to your website as possible. Get links by writing content for other blogs or website, writing bits or articles for newspaper and on-line magazines. Get featured in magazines and newspapers and have them list your website with a live link. Also, register with HARO which stands for Help A Reporter Out. Your tips that you share on your area of expertise may get picked up and shared with thousands of readers. They see your website link, and check out what other pearls of wisdom you have to share.

Joe Howard, Senior Marketing Manager at Masslight, Washington DC

(www.josephhirschhornhoward.com)
421. Expert Roundups Can Work Wonders

Your priority when it comes to SEO really depends on the purpose of your website, but my best piece of advice would be to focus on producing great content that features those who are authorities in your industry. Most SEOs focus on producing content that simply tries to rank for a single, specific keyword phrase - it's much more effective to feature other experts in your industry, share your content with them, and use them to help share your content across the Web. That will help you increase high-quality traffic (and backlinks) coming to your site, which in turn will grow your list of email subscribers and your website's influence.

Robert Lee, CEO of Circa Interactive (www.circainteractiveseo.com)

422. Look at trends over the long term, not day-to-day fluctuations.

What is your number one SEO tip?
Rankings will change, but if you over-analyze day-to-day fluctuations then you will drive yourself crazy and possibly make poor decisions regarding optimization techniques.

Utilizing a long-term approach can help SEO's see recurring patterns and trends, which will enable them to make strategic decisions regarding their SEO strategies. SEO (and specifically link building) is a long term digital marketing approach. The days of the SEO quick fix are gone.

What is your number one content marketing tip?
Produce great content and position it in front of audiences that can build you links. Introducing a social strategy that produces brand mentions and shares is good, but too often SEOs expect a strong social presence to return strong rankings.
While there is a relationship between strong
rankings and effective social media, one does not guarantee the other.

Place your content in front of bloggers and digital publishers that are relevant and that you know will feature your content. Tie it to a current event or relate it to an existing piece on their website, and most editors or bloggers will be at least be willing to give you some type of feedback, which could be the beginning of a relationship.

What is your best strategy to gaining more traffic?
Focus on the long-tail. While the various keyword tools are useful at understanding search volume on a high level, they sometimes miss

opportunities when it comes to longer tail searches that could be extremely relevant to your client's product or service. To find these keywords, take a look at Webmaster Tools or a search query report within an advertising campaign; they can sometimes reveal hidden gems.

CHAPTER 12
Common SEO Myths

There's a lot of information out there, and practically anyone can make up information. A lot of it has changed, and a lot of it is complete garbage. This is the very section where you get to learn of *what is just **not** working SEO*. Listen carefully. I've included some myths myself, and I've also asked a lot of SEO experts and digital marketing consultants to chip their thoughts in also.

A lot of these myths have been uttered by SEO experts and clients who go to SEO agencies. You'd be surprised. The heading of each myth is a ***myth*** and not a ***tip***. Keep that in mind.

Here we go!

423. Domain Age Still Matters
It used to be important, back in the days when you still found websites that looked like they were built in the 90s. Today though, the age of your domain doesn't matter at all.
Provided you have a solid website with solid content, you have just as good a chance as any websites built ten years ago. Don't pay attention to domain age, it's a worthless metric these days.

424. The More Pages You Have, The More Authority Your Site Has
The common myth is that the more pages you have, the more authority your site gets and the more Google will trust you.
However, it's certainly true that the more quality pages you have, the more traffic you get. But without backlinks, you won't build any authority. In short, quality pages and backlinks build authority, and not only one without the other. Having just thin pages with backlinks is spam, and having pages with no backlinks is only going to lead to a stale website.

There's no need to go building up hundreds of blog posts and sales pages about your company, because you won't build your authority at all. The only way to build authority is through receiving links from highly trusted and reputable websites and blogs.

CHAPTER 12: COMMON SEO MYTHS

Take Backlinko for example, which is an SEO blog and ranks first, second and third for highly competitive keywords such as "linkbuilding", "keyword research" and "seo tips". Brian Dean, the founder, has only written 21 blog posts.

Not 200 or 2000.

Just 21.

The reason why he is ranking so well for those keywords is because he aced his linkbuilding, and got backlinks from high PR websites and blogs. His 21 blog posts are also "monster posts", ie: posts that are well over 8000 words long and are filled with screenshots, case studies and insanely useful tips.

Google recognised this, and that's why his website turned from a blank Wordpress installation to a hugely successful websites in a highly competitive space.

The lesson learned here is that you should create evergreen, insanely helpful content which you can get people to link to in the years ahead, rather than hundreds of pages that offer little value.

425. Google Don't Like .NET or .INFO Websites

The myth is that Google favors the ".com" domain extension, and thinks that the .net and .info domain extensions are spammy, thus, they should rank lower. Even though ".com" websites are more common not just on the web but in search results, Google doesn't discriminate websites just because their domain extensions are ".net", ".co", ".io" or ".info". If you own a website with one of the lesser known domain extensions, don't give in to the myth that you will be ranked lower.

426. Get The Website Launched First, Then Start Your SEO

The common scenario that agencies get:
Client approaches an SEO agency and says, *"Please SEO this page"* or *"Add some SEO pizazz to our homepage".*
SEO used to work like that, where you could just build links through blog networks, Fiverr and link farms. Add some keyword stuffing and you'd rank in a couple of weeks!

Not today though.

For the last few years, SEO has become a plan or a strategy before a website is even built. That means planning what keywords to target, what domain name to choose, what content to write, what influencers to target, where to get backlinks in a Google-friendly way. All this has to then be integrated with the website, and has to become seamless with the overall website design.

So, don't ever start a website in the future without planning your SEO strategy.

427. Build A New Website, If You Haven't Planned Your SEO

If you have started a website, and you only realize lately that you should have planned an SEO strategy *before* you built your website – don't feel too bad.

You can still work on your SEO, but it may require rewriting a few pages for optimal keyword targeting and a bit of chopping and changing. However, don't get too disheartened. Just use the tips in this book, and your rankings will start improving very soon!

428. Everyone Gets Different Search Results, So A Solid Ranking Doesn't Exist Anymore

This is partly true but is still a myth.

Because of personalization, everyone sees different results pages because of their interests, previous search history and location. For me a search of "pink" results in "pink floyd" ranking second because

I've searched them before and Google knows I have an interest in them. If you were a fan of Pink, the pop singer, the results would be completely different.

However, that's not to mean that *every* single set of search results is different. This mainly applies to results which can be personalized such as location based queries and head keywords (dog, pink, broad keywords). For long tail keywords, there can be a results page which is the same for everyone. Sure, there might be a few tweaks but overall, the search results will stay solid enough.

CHAPTER 12: COMMON SEO MYTHS

429. Spending Money On Paid Search Raises Your Organic Rankings –
This myth is still being popularized all over the web. It's believed that if you worship Google by paying for advertising, they might give you a heads up on the organic rankings too.
It's a nice idea, but is nothing more than a fantasy.

430. Social Media Signals Have An Effect On Your SEO
Yes, social media can impact your SEO *indirectly* by bringing more links and traffic to your website, resulting in more backlinks in the long term or even, getting a feature by a journalist.
But Google have officially announced that social media signals are not a part of their ranking algorithm.

There's been a lot of speculation on whether these signals really matter. Some say that because of Hummingbird algorithm change, social media signals have become more important whilst others dismiss the idea entirely. I, for one, have to take Google's final say on this – social media signals are not taken into consideration when ranking a website.
Expect this to change though, in the coming years.
So if your post goes viral on social media, and you get a boost in the rankings, it's probably because other websites have linked to your website or you got a mention by other bloggers – not because it got 20,000 shares on social media.

You may have noticed me talking a lot about going viral on social media, and optimizing content for social media shares. This is not because of a direct impact on SEO, but more a way of getting more backlinks and mentions to your website. When niche influencers see that you have written popular content, they will allow you to write guest posts or will link to your posts.

431. Your Homepage Needs A Lot of Content
The myth is that you need pages of content on your homepage, just because you might get penalized for "poor quality content".
The truth is that homepages are "looked at" differently to a blog post or sales page. Homepages need some content but not a huge amount. Take a look at some killer homepages and you'll see that they contain at most, a couple of sentences or paragraphs.

Include all the necessary content you need, but don't expand your page with worthless content that could be placed somewhere else just because Google might "rank you higher".

432. If You Link To Other Sites, Your Page Loses PageRank

This myth is a little complicated to demystify, but here's basically why your site doesn't lose PageRank when it links to other sites.

Let's say your homepage has a PR of 4. It links to a page on Wikipedia, thus giving some of its PageRank to the Wikipedia page. But it still retains the PageRank that it had before it gave a link to Wikipedia.

In short, the PageRank on your page will stay the same even if you link to a bunch of other sites, because the PageRank flows through the links, but you will still retain the same amount.

What The Experts Say

Krystian Szastok, Digital Marketing Manager At Rocketmill (www.rocketmill.co.uk)

433. Linkbuilding is dead

The myth I hate the most is that 'link building is dead'.

SO many say SEO is dead and link building is dead, yet the most successful ranking sites do SEO and link building.

They are however doing it in a modern way that's in line with Google's guidelines, by creating great content and attracting natural links that come as ang effect.

Dylan Kissane, Content Manager at DOZ (www.doz.com)

434. Social media will improve your rankings

One SEO myth that drives me crazy is a focus on social media to the detriment of strong site content. Whether social media sites take over good old fashioned content marketing as the most important aspect of true SEO remains to be seen, but for the time being it should just be considered another cog in a bigger SEO machine.

Social media remains a means of backing up and delivering visitors to interesting content on your site - it is not a 'magic SEO bullet' that will lift your Google rankings all by itself.

James Rice, Head of Digital Marketing at Wikijob (www.wikijob.co.uk)

434. Meta keywords are useful

My pet hate is the idea that meta keywords are useful. Meta keywords are a type of HTML tag where you can specify particular keyword phrases the page is targeted for. Years ago, these were a fundamental part of on-page optimization (the idea being you could flag keywords not actually on the page, to help search engines to classify the page's content). But then it all got very spammy, very quickly. Google, Bing and most other search engines now completely disregards these keywords. In fact, there are two reasons why having no meta keywords is better than having any:

1. They indicate to search engines what keywords to penalize the page for if manipulation is observed;
2. Your competitors can easily see what keywords you are targeting.

Michael Davies, Founder of Owltutors.com (www.owltutors.co.uk)

434. Create meta data for every single page on your website

An SEO myth I hate is that you need to provide meta-data for every page on your website. I've met many people who believe they should be creating meta descriptions, SEF URLs and enticing title tags for EVERY page on their site. Whilst this is a great idea for content you want to be found for, it isn't necessary for any nuts and bolts pages on your site that don't need to be found though organic search: contact forms, terms and conditions pages etc.

Dan Smith, SEO Specialist at Leighton (www.leighton.com)

435. Ranking for certain keywords is a measure of success

The most notable myth for me (assuming we're ignoring the common backlinks no longer work-type myths) has got to be the belief that ranking for keywords is a primary metric for SEO success.

Monitoring keyword rankings was once a great indication your SEO strategy was successful, but today, it's much more beneficial - and valuable - to look at organic traffic and conversions. After all, increasing these is what the true end goal is.

Scott Kiwovitz, Community and Blog Wrangler at Photocrati (www.photocrati.com)

436. Blogging by itself will get you ranking better

One myth that I too often hear photographers conversing about is the idea that blogging will get them to rank better. In a way that myth is true, but it's not as simple as that.

The simple act of blogging, on its own, will not do much for search engine rankings. However, blogging with strategic optimization in the metadata, schema markup, the actual content and of course the images as well is what will go into helping a website rank
better.

Jacky Chou, Founder of Indexy (www.indexy.com)

437. You don't need links

The myth that you don't need links, ticks me off. Large sites have teams of outreach people that contact bloggers and editors daily looking to drop links, and links win. They are the biggest signal Google takes into consideration.

CHAPTER 12: COMMON SEO MYTHS

Don't believe anything else. Smart link building is where it's at. You want to be able to look at your links and be confident that if a Google employee saw the link they wouldn't look twice because it appears as natural as it gets.

You need links. You will always need links to rank. Content and onsite optimization are all important parts of SEO but nothing will ever replace the importance of links. You have to be very smart when building links or if you hire a SEO company you want to make sure they know what they are doing and aren't building links just for the sake of building a link to throw it into a report!

Bas van den Beld, 'State of Digital' Founder (www.stateofdigital.com)

438. *SEO is all about optimizing for search engines*

I hate the myth that SEO is about optimizing for search engines, it's not, it's optimizing for humans. The people that are doing the search queries are the most important. Answer their questions and you will not just be able to rank better, it will convert better. In the end SEO is about the audience you are trying to reach, not the search engine.

Keith Browning, SEO Specialist At Ireland Hotels (www.irelandhotels.com)

439. *Domain names are no longer important*

The SEO myth I hate, which I'm constantly being told, is that domain names are no longer important.

I can tell from firsthand experience that this is not true! Domain name makes a very significant difference. Not only are we ranked number 1 on Google for "Ireland Hotels" in almost all geographic locations but we immediately rank number 1 or very high for any terms that contain Ireland and hotels. This can happen even when we don't really follow a lot of the other basic SEO rules.

Jacob Stempniewicz: Vice President, Marketing at Andovar (www.andovar.com)

440. Do SEO once and you're done

The SEO myth I hate the most is that you only need to do SEO once and you're done. Truth is - you'll only see sustained results if you invest on-going effort into SEO on a long-term basis.
This means two things:

1. Every time you update or publish something, you should make sure it is SEO-optimized
2. Stay on top of latest tips and tricks and search engine updates, which may require you to tweak your old content.

Teodora Vingan, SEO Analyst at Squirrly (www.squirrly.co)

441. If you produce content, you don't need links

The one SEO myth that I'm quite sick of is the fact that you don't need link building for a website that produces content. This is a myth that was recently busted (even if people were still debating around this topic) by Neil Patel in an article where he showed the fact that your articles are nothing if you don't build links to your website.

The takeaway is that a good title, with keywords, and an awesome article will not skyrocket in Google search results, nor will your website be on the first page of Google. Link build your way to get the best results.

Matthew Jonas, President of TopFire Media (www.topfiremedia.com)

442. A newly launched website will start ranking in a day

The SEO myth that really gets under my skin is the fallacy that a newly launched website will appear on the first page of Google search the next day.

This is simply unrealistic. New websites have to be indexed by the search

CHAPTER 12: COMMON SEO MYTHS

engine (Google), and while you can help the process through strong website structure, a high amount of inbound links, and optimizing your site with SEO rich keywords, there isn't a set time for your website to be indexed.

It can take up to 30 days for Google to index new websites. While it may be shorter, don't expect your new website to appear on page one of a Google search after 24 hours.

Ron Perry, CEO of egniteBIZ (www.egnite.biz)
443. Submitting your site to a search engine will increase your rankings

The myth surrounding search engine submission is a popular one. Basically,
the idea is that submitting your site or pages to the search engines will increase your rankings. However, this is not true. The fact of the matter is that all it will do is simply notify the search engines to look at content/pages they would have found on their own assuming that your site is
built correctly.

Submitting your site to search engines may nominally reduce the time it take for your page to get indexed but it will not help your rankings.

Ashley Orndorff, Director of Marketing at Paradox Labs (www.paradoxlabs.com)
444. Getting the number one spot is all that matters

The SEO myth that ticks me off the most is that getting the #1 spot in Google is all that matters (and that SEO alone will get you there, cheaply). Being able to say you're #1 in Google for X can be great for your business, but it's not the end-all, be-all for you.

187

The search algorithms are always adjusting and always changing - your rankings will fluctuate, no matter what you do. Plus, once you focus so much on where you're ranking for one keyword or query, you lose sight of all the other opportunities available to you. What about that long-tail keyword on the second or third page that will drive more conversions for you? Why not focus on improving your visibility around that subject?

I've seen it time and time again. Some site owners become so focused on being #1 for X that they don't realize the query they're chasing is purely vanity and doesn't even drive the majority of their revenue; let alone that it's so competitive, they won't even be able to break into the top 5 without a massive amount of time and investment.

Sorry, not sorry, you're not going to be able to beat out Amazon and Wal-Mart with minimal effort and no budget.

If you want to have higher visibility over established brands much more authoritative and trusted than you, it's going to take a lot of effort, a lot of time, and, most importantly, a lot of very intelligent strategy. If you want to outrank them on realistic, relevant topics, you're going to have to outmaneuver them - and with a strong, multichannel, integrated approach.

Brittany Berger, Digital Content Supervisor at eZanga (www.brittanyberger.com)

445. Meta descriptions don't matter

The SEO myth I hate is that meta descriptions don't matter. Just because they're not a ranking factor, doesn't mean they don't matter. Search engine optimization should cover the entire process involved in earning search traffic, not just appearing on the results page. Once your listing shows up, you still need to get the searcher to click. That's where meta descriptions come in. It's your chance to draw them in and stand out from the other results on the page.

Roxel Gestiada, Junior Specialist in Business Development at Infinit Outsourcing (www.infinit-o.com)

446. Linkbuilding is dead

One SEO myth that I really hate is about link building being dead. This is actually not the case. Link building will always be a part of SEO. The only thing that changed about it is the whole process. Google aims to make link building as natural as possible.

Hence, the combination of Panda and Penguin updates. White-hat link building is still effective. However, Google is now particular when it comes to exact match keywords. The bottom line is, natural link building should be observed.

John Jones, Digital Marketing & Communications Manager at USA Financial

447. SEO can be done quickly, and if you pay the money – you'll get to the top

One of the SEO myths or misconceptions that always frustrates me often comes from high level executives of companies that want to better search results for their name or product. The question is frequently, *"How much do we have to pay Google to get 'good' search results?"*.

The reality, that takes a long while for them to understand, is that SEO requires time and persistence. It's not something that can be fixed in 20 minutes with one solution like a leaky faucet.

Andrew Akesson, Senior Technical SEO at VennDigital (www.venndigital.co.uk)

448. Get only one link per domain

When SEO's are link prospecting and see that they already have a link from their target domain, so they don't proceed any further, as they feel they should get a link on a new/different domain, just so they can have more referring domains pointing to their site. Two things that really annoy me about this are:
- Pages have their own authority (which speaks for itself really) get a link on a page of a high performing domain and that authority can be passed through to yours.
- Referral traffic is (in my mind) a great indicator of a good link. If you have a link on bbc.co.uk and it brought through 10,000 referral visits to your site, why wouldn't you approach that site again with a new outreach idea and get another set of high number referrals to your site?

William Bauer, Managing Director at Royce Leather Gifts (www.royceleathergifts.com)

449. Keyword stuff your content, it still works

Keywords do help, but you have to use them wisely. You have to be careful not to overuse them. Otherwise, you could be penalized for keyword stuffing.

Also - focus on longer keywords in your writing. People today search by phrases and not single words. Instead of just searching for *"luggage store"* they search for *"best luggage store in Manhattan"*. By using longer keyword phrases, you make it easier for people to find you by having less competition for the same phrase. You also help yourself by attracting more of your target customers and less generic traffic.

Jasmine Davis, Client Engagement Manager at Community Elf (www.communityelf.com)

450. Use keywords exactly as written

You definitely don't have to use keywords exactly as written. Even today, I'll get clients who insist that their keywords or phrases must be included exactly as written.

While it was a fun challenge, it also restricted what you could write and occasionally, you'd get a keyword with literally no natural use. Fortunately, you can use keywords today in modified forms, with punctuation, and even broken up by other words - it's more about the overall theme of a page. Keywords still matter, don't get me wrong - but a specific keyword is not the end-all, be-all of SEO strategy.

Leigh Wendinger, Lead Inbound Marketing Specialist at FUN.com

451. If you create great content, the rest will all fall into place

Sure, if you create great content you have a leg up on the competition. However, content won't benefit you unless you share it or have a following like the Huffington Post. The SEO world has shifted from link building to link earning with increasing amounts of content, but you still need successful outreach campaigns to bridge that gap and make your efforts successful.

Stephen Murphy, CMO of Red Bamboo Marketing (www.redbamboomarketing.com)

452. Search traffic volume equals success

At the end of the day, we have to measure SEO traffic based on intent and conversions. Ignore broad based keywords that may send boat loads of traffic, but may not be qualified traffic that is looking to buy your products or services.

For example, a company that sells analytics dashboards may want to focus on a term like "big data software tools" (a keyword with purchase intent) vs. a broad term like "big data", a keyword that might be more research driven.

My advice: Measure your success by SEO traffic that hits qualified pages (pricing, products, etc.) and/or converts into leads. Focusing on this traffic will give you a greater bang for your buck with your SEO strategy and lead to more meaningful results.

Graham Onak, Marketing Specialist at GainTap (www.gaintap.com)

453. The Yoast Wordpress Plug-in Will Do All Your SEO For You

The myth I hate is that Yoast's SEO plugin for WordPress is like an SEO specialist in a box. I've had clients mention that they don't need SEO help because they have the plugin installed and enter an SEO Keyword to optimize for their pages.

But the plugin doesn't help unless you know how it functions. For example the SEO Keyword simply checks the number of times the keyword is used on the webpage. It isn't really optimizing for it. Great plugin, but not an SEO specialist replacement. There's a lot more that goes into SEO than that.

Peter Moeller, Marketing Director at Scarinci Hollenbeck (www.scarincihollenbeck.com)

454. You can do SEO in a certain time frame

Companies that put time frames on their SEO as a selling point. I'll get you to the first page of google in three months. THAT IS NOT SEO! And if you are sold by this crap, do yourself a favor and use the free tools provided by Google to see how many people actually search for the term you are now ranking for in Google. I guarantee you it's not worth your money.

I also hate when people say Google is moving away from keywords. Listen, no matter how much we want to believe keywords are dead, I and everyone else with an internet connection uses Google for our search queries; and we always put the KEY words we are looking for. I don't search *frog* when I want to know *Ben & Jerry's newest ice-cream flavor*. I search *what is Ben and Jerry's newest ice cream flavors*.

Brandon Seymour, Beymour Consulting (www.beymour.com)

455. EMDs are not valuable anymore

One thing I hear all the time from SEOs and online marketers is that exact-match domains (EMDs) no longer have any influence on search rankings.

I've worked with clients in several highly competitive industries, and I can tell you from personal experience that EMDs still work for SEO. Back in September of 2012, Google released their EMD Update which aimed to prevent poor quality sites from ranking well simply because they use a keyword-rich domain name. Although some sites may have been hit, I still see plenty of low quality sites ranking in the top 3 positions for highly competitive terms.
Many of these sites have weak back-link profiles, thin or duplicate content and a relatively low domain authority (when compared to sites ranked lower for the same terms). The only possible reason that they're currently ranking is because of their domain.

Liz Mazzei, Marketing Consultant (www.lizmazzei.com)

456. Guest blogging is dead

I hate when people say that guest blogging isn't good for SEO. Wrong! The more REAL and NATURAL links to your site from other pages the better.

Sean Malseed, Founder of CircleRank and Frequent Speaker at SMX (www.circlerank.com)

457. Get the right traffic, by focusing on specific keywords that'll convert more

My beloved new client says "Our primary goal is to rank for X keyword ASAP". Well client, I like you a lot and I care about your business, so let me tell you a story. I had a client selling gaming computers, who really wanted to rank number one for gaming computers with 40,500 monthly searches.

I bluntly, and with the offering of a nice cold beer, told them that this is waste all of your time and money. The goal of your site is not get all traffic - it's *conversions, money, and profit.*
Are people searching gaming computers really looking to buy right now?

Who knows... maybe they're looking for a definition. Or reviews. Or a how-to guide to build their own. Or Best Buy's computer department phone number. Everything has a purchase funnel, and you want to be represented when people are ready to BUY. Spread those keywords out.

Want proof? Here's proof. I did a quick search on gaming computer related keywords. It literally took me two seconds to find 798 related keywords that also include the word *buy* in it. The combined search volume for these keywords is 70,680 - almost twice that of the single keyword you were coveting.

So you tell me - would you rather have 40,500 tire-kickers and "should , shouldn't I" people see your site, or would you rather be seen by 70,680 who are looking to buy a computer right now?

The moral of the story: Keyword research takes research. Keep an open mind, and dig in.

Matthew Sommer, Chief Strategic Officer at Brolik (www.brolik.com)

458. You can beat Google, you just need to do it right

The #1 worst, most destructive myth I have heard repeatedly is "I beat Google". This is just ridiculous. It shows that you are thinking about SEO in absolutely the wrong way. At the beginning search engines were very rudimentary, you could increase your ranking for a search term just by placing it more often on the page than your competitor.

This led to people making text the same color as the background that just says the term over and over again. Then it was stuffing meta tags. Then link building networks. These were all attempts to game the system. They worked for a time, until engines like Google got wise to the technique and changed their algorithms to counteract.

This is a continual game of cat and mouse. With the considerable brain trust and resources that Google has at this point, I can confidently tell you that you will never win. Maybe for a few weeks or months, but they will catch up, and will very likely penalize your site for these activities. Instead, you have to work with search engines to help them accomplish their goal - To provide the best, most relevant results for users' queries.

This idea won't bring you the immediate boosts of rank or traffic that some black hat techniques will, but it will help to provide a genuine, lasting presence on search engines that will do far more good for your business than trying to game the system.

Casandra Campbell, Minimalist Marketing (www.casandracampbell.com)

459. Nofollow links have no value, and anchor text doesn't matter

1. I hate the myth that nofollow links have no value! Just because they're not passing link juice' doesn't mean they're not helping you. Nofollow links are an important part of a well-rounded (read: trustworthy) link profile. I know plenty of people who have ranked websites with nothing more than blog comments and Wikipedia citations.

2. Another myth which annoys me is that anchor text doesn't matter. Just Google "click here" and see what comes up. Huge authority websites like Paypal and Adobe are ranking for the term click here not because they're targeting it, but because they have tons of links pointing at them with that very anchor text.

Ryan Freman, Founder of Strider SEO (www.striderseo.com)

460. "A Number 1 Ranking Is The Key To Riches & Success"

While ranking highly for any search term is a worthwhile goal, more than rank needs to be considered:

1. Am I ranking for the right terms? A flood of irrelevant traffic to your site will hurt more than help. Some more specific terms will drive many more conversions than short generic terms. Do the research before targeting search phrases.

2. Ranking is relative. Search results reflect various degrees of personalization, so while you may see yourself ranking in a certain position for your searches customers in different areas, with different search histories, can be seeing remarkably different results.

3. Focus on goals, not rank: Ranking is a means to an end. If your site experience is lousy, your bottom line won't improve by moving from #8 to #3 in the search results. Set goals like relevant traffic, increasing measurable engagement, micro conversions page to page, and tangible conversions like sales or subscriptions.

Ron Johnson, Marketing Director at CyberOptik (www.cyberoptik.net)

461. The more links you've got, the higher you'll rank

This is the myth I hate the most: "The more links pointing to your website the better, no matter what the links are."
Link quality is important, one quality link is much more valuable than a bunch of garbage links.

Mary Bowling, Ignitor Digital (www.ignitordigital.com)

462. Local SEO is easy

Many people think that local SEO is easy. It used to be back in the day, but now it is even more complex. To be successful in ranking in the local packs and localized organic results, one must now master both organic SEO and local SEO.

Sherry Holub, Creative Director at JV Media Design (www.jvmediadesign.com)

463. "We already did SEO"

I hate it when a client says, "We already did SEO" - DID being the operative word here. A lot of people are under the impression that if they pay an SEO company to optimize their website, they're done and they don't have to worry about it anymore.

This myth is so totally wrong. SEO is not something you do once and forget about. It's actually an on-going process with a million and one variables that need to be adjusted and finessed on an on-going basis. Just the fact that Google is continually changing their metrics should put the fear into anyone who thinks they can just do it once.

Erin Cunningham, Assistant Account Executive at Lotus823 (www.lotus823.com)

464. SEO is dead

SEO is *not* dead. If you're still using SEO the way you were five, ten years ago it's not going to be as effective today. SEO has changed and you need to change the tactics you're using as well. There is so much more to SEO than keywords in 2015. While keywords still matter, content marketing, social media and public relations should all be integrated with your SEO strategy.

Jason White, VP of SEO and SEM at Dragon Search Marketing (www.dragonsearchmarketing.com)

465. "Please SEO this"

When someone says "please SEO this".
You can't just SEO something. Optimization has many considerations and spans many types of communications. SEO itself is a myth; often an educated
best guess. SEO's have a unique ability to increase the reach and findability of many different communications and platforms. Actions are often small but they accumulate and cannot be confined to a single action.

Bria Burk, Digital Marketing Manager at Androvett (www.androvett.com)

466. SEO is about the latest technical methods to game the system

The goal of a search engine is to understand what the user needs and to provide the right search results to answer their questions. While it is true that search engines look at hundreds of factors when ranking a site, the best long-term strategy to generating business through search is to create great content that users want to read.

Compared to AltaVista in the '90s, search engines are now far better at interpreting the intent of search queries and filtering out the online spam. Search engine optimization is shifting to become more about building online relationships through content, and less about technical strategies to game the system.

To put it simply, if you want business from users via search results, find out what users want to know, and spend the time creating content that will answer their questions.

Kent Lewis, Founder of Anvil Media (www.anvilmedia.com)

467. SEO is all about embedding keywords and building links

Here is my most hated SEO myth:

"SEO is all about embedding keywords into copy and code and building a few inbound links. It's relatively simple to get into Google's good graces."

I've told my clients that Google is not about cracking their monumental technology or algorithms, but about doing good marketing. If you build a site that people enjoy surfing and fill it with useful content, visitors will talk about it and Google will reward you.

CHAPTER 13

SEO Philosophy

There are a few rules in SEO that you just need to get right. These are general rules that span across all aspects of SEO. Make sure you follow them, and understand them fully.

Follow these rules and you shall become an SEO master.

A little philosophy killed no one, right?

468. Be Patient

You probably know this already, but it's worth mentioning again. SEO takes months to work, to see any results whatsoever. You build links today and you sow the seeds for future success. Most clients think that they can rank well in a week, or even in a month. You won't see real results for months. Just be patient. It takes time, but when the time comes – you will be rewarded very generously for it.

469. Think Outside The Box

The most unique website will win the most votes. Those that can come up with the most unique linkbuilding techniques are going to win in the rankings. SEO these days is all about thinking outside the box. Who thought that getting a link on another website could get so creative? There's guest blogging, fixing broken links, pointing out hacked pages, updating old content and so much more. All those techniques stemmed from creativity.

Think creatively because there are hundreds of SEO techniques out there that you can come up with, that no one else has used. All you have to do is think differently to the rest of us.

470. Be Committed

Keep at it. Most webmasters stop just when they're about to become successful.

One of the most difficult things to do in SEO is to stay committed. It's very easy to get it started in an enthusiastic manner, and then the enthusiasm starts to wane as the days go by.

CHAPTER 13: SEO PHILOSOPHY

Don't let your enthusiasm wane, keep it up! Just imagine your Google Analytics graph soaring into the thousands and then, hundreds of thousands of views every day.

471. Throw Yourself Into SEO Like You Mean It

You can't fake it. It's either all or nothing. SEO is one of those things that just has to be fully worked at, or not at all. You make the decision. If you want results, you've got to look at every aspect of SEO and implement it on your website.

SEO is also an ongoing thing. Every new page you publish will have to be optimized for SEO and the same for every blog post. You'll always have to build new links. You'll always have to make your site faster, and check it technically. It's a lot of work, so make the decision to do it properly, rather than half-heartedly.

472. Be Passionate About Your Website

Embrace your website, your work and what you do. Believe it or not, but that passion and enthusiasm will actually show results. Love what you do, and the rest will follow. Enthusiasm is infectious and people will pick up on your website, if they see that you love what you do.

473. Remember That Humans Buy, Not Search Engines

It's easy to get sidetracked and start developing only with the search engine in mind, and not the user. Search engines aren't the ones to pay you money or give you a phone call or click on your ads. People do. So always remember to put people first, before anything else.

474. Keep Yourself Updated

Whilst SEO may appear to be timeless, it's always changing. Every year, SEO has changed a lot from the thing it used to be a year ago. Keep yourself updated, because I guarantee you, this time next year SEO will be slightly different.

If you don't manipulate the search results with short lived tricks, you'll find that your SEO work will stand the test of time. SEO is never going to change hugely so that the links you build today or the keywords you target will no longer be relevant. But there will always be tiny tweaks that you'll still need to watch out for.

The best way to keep yourself updated is by subscribing to SEO news websites such as Search Engine Land, Search Engine Watch and Moz. In addition, this book will always be updated should there be any need.

475. Don't Ignore Content Marketing
Content marketing is the fundamental pillar which will build your brand, get you known on social media and bring you traffic.

It doesn't matter what niche you're in because there will be an audience for your content somewhere in the world. Don't make excuses and ignore content marketing, because you don't consider yourself a writer or that your website is in a "boring" (a niche not many people know about, or don't really want to read about) or hugely competitive niche. Unless you're a local business and you get most of your leads from notices on local noticeboards, there is a need to build content. If you want more money, you've got to start investing in content creation.

476. You Need Conversion Too
There's no use getting thousands of daily hits when all that converts to zero sales and zero profit. Just like how SEO is a vital part of your website's success, so is conversion.
Again, just like SEO, conversion is a whole science. There are entire books, websites, blogs and tools related to conversion. The best websites I recommend for conversion include Unbounce, Crazy Egg and Optimizely. You might find that your website converts extremely well without learning the exact science. It really depends on your niche, but conversion definitely has to be integrated into your digital marketing strategy.

477. Update Your Best Performing Pages
Updating your best performing pages can give you a boost in the rankings. On HubPages, an article directory, they have updated their articles and have seen a 20% increase in traffic to these articles. Check your highest earning pages in terms of traffic and update them. You can update them by adding new text, images, statistics and multimedia. Whatever updates you make, be sure to expect a nice boost in traffic.

CHAPTER 13: SEO PHILOSOPHY

478. Build Relationships

SEO is turning from manipulating search engines to developing relationships with niche influencers. For promotion, link building and so much more – you will need to build relationships with key influencers in your niche.

These people could have thousands of followers on social media, be influential bloggers or just people that we all look up to. Whoever it is, make sure to reach out to them by commenting on their blog, letting them know you appreciate their work, and following them on social media. It's corny, but it works.

As Keith Ferazzi (author of "Never Eat Alone") once said, *"Build your network before you need it"*.

479. No More Manipulation

I've said it before and I'll say it again. Always be a white hat SEO, and never go to the dark side. There are no shortcuts to SEO anymore. It's either full on persistence or nothing. So no matter how tempted you are to get more traffic through black hat manipulation and tricks, don't give in. Too many webmasters already did, and they now suffer the consequences.

480. Use Evernote, It's Indispensable

I only started using Evernote recently, and it really enhanced my productivity. In case you haven't heard of it yet, Evernote is basically an app for all your devices where you can write notes, clip webpages, take screenshots and organize all that into notebooks. A lot of people use Evernote to record any ideas that strike them at a particular moment, but then when they try to remember that idea later on, they can't remember.

I strongly believe that by using Evernote, you can enhance your SEO results. Here, you can record potential keyword ideas, set reminders for linkbuilding, innovation ideas for your website or clip any interesting findings from the web. It works on all your devices (desktop and mobile), and is especially useful on the go. If you're going to download a life-changing app this year, it's got to be Evernote. (www.evernote.com)

481. Offer Something Insanely Useful

If your website doesn't provide any value to your readers, there's no point doing any SEO at all. You need to attract your readers to subscribing to your blog, trying your products and make them become interested. But if your blog doesn't offer anything useful to them, you might as well pack up. There is a demand for anything and everything online, so be the one to answer that call.

482. Remember Your Website's Values

Always stick to the core of what your website is all about. Don't create off-topic content just because it's popular at the moment or build links from off-topic websites just because the opportunity arose. Make decisions based on your website's niche and values.

483. "The Difference Between Try and Triumph Is Just A Little Umph" – Unknown

You need that something extra special to get your website on a popular scale. It could be that your products are cheaper than everyone else's or that your blog posts are so actionable that nobody else can compete. It's difficult to do SEO if you don't have that extra spark that people want. Find the unique thing about your company or website and emphasise it on your home page, outreach, PR and so on. That is what will separate your website from the crowd.

484. "Great content is the best sales tool in the world" – Marcus Sherdian

We're sick of advertising. The only way to get the unwashed masses excited about your brand or products is through content. Help them first, and then they'll respond a lot better than you think.

485. "What you do after you create your content is what truly counts"- Gary Vaynerchuk

You can create content all day, but if you don't actually promote it, nothing exciting happens. Promotion is what everyone wants, but can't seem to get it. SEO is the best, and perhaps the cheapest way to get thousands of people to view your site daily. That's why working towards page one is essential, and the only way to do that is through linkbuilding.

CHAPTER 13: SEO PHILOSOPHY

486. "There is no black magic to successfully attracting customers via the web" – Rand Fishkin
If that was the case, you'd find me splurging all my innermost black magic secrets in this book. There are none.

487. In this age of micro blogging and two second sound bites, almost no one has the attention span or time to read more than a few sentences" – Tim Frick
Great titles. Great sales copy. Be quick about it and use words which evoke a response or a click.

488. "The only way to win at content marketing is for the reader to say, 'This was written specifically for me'" – Jamie Turner
Did you ever read an article, when you were on wits end, and it solved your problem or question? It feels like that article was written only for you. I remember getting a nasty virus on my computer and couldn't remove it. There were no removal guides on the internet, and nobody seemed to have heard of it. I was getting extremely worried, since the virus was wreaking havoc across my files and documents.

But then, I stumbled across an article by Computer which was particularly about that virus, and step by step – showed me how to remove it. I tried the steps, and sure enough, the virus was removed. I'll never forget the relief and the way I looked up to that website again.
When you evoke that indescribable feeling in a reader, magical things will happen.

489. "Content is the reason search began in the first place" – Lee Odden
There would be no Google if it wasn't for content. Now that's saying something.

490. "The best marketing doesn't feel like marketing" – Tom Fishburne
Telemarketing, TV advertising and radio advertising *feels* like marketing. It's tedious, nobody listens to it and even if they do, the sheer cost of that advertising will make quite an unforgettable dent in your bank account. Compare this to SEO where you can expect fantastic results by doing it in a creative and non-tedious way. And if you're an internet lover, it doesn't really feel like work.

491. "Traditional marketing is telling the world you're a rock star. Content marketing is showing you are one" – Robert Rose

Traditional marketing brings happiness to its creators and tears to its audience. Content brings happiness to its creators and happiness to its audience. That's the difference. Showing people that you can write and be a rockstar on the internet at the same time, is a whole lot better than hogging the newspaper, TV or radio.

492. "The future of content marketing is in your hands" – David Hahn

Get creative and re-invent the wheel. Content marketing can become anything you want it to be, if you imagine it.

493. "When you enchant people, your goal is not to make money from them or to get them to do what you want, but to fill them with great delight." – Guy Kawasaki

Make it look like you actually want to enchant your readers with content. Once they're a fan of your content, they'll buy your products and become true customers.

494. "My theory is that in the age of the internet, it's what you write not where you write it that matters" – Dan Lyons

It doesn't matter who you are or where you write. With the right content and promotion, you can get that content to span across the world, and reach readers in places you've never imagined.

495. "Google only loves you when everyone else loves you first" – Wendy Piersall

Create a website that will entice, convert and engage. If you have a website, make sure your products stand out from the rest. Once you have a solid foundation, your SEO will become a whole lot easier.

496. "If you wait until there is another case study in your industry, you will be too late" – Seth Godin

Start working on your SEO now. There's no time like the present, after all.

497. "The paradox is the more info you give away, the more people will buy what you have to give" Brian Clark

Strange, but true. The more content your give to people for free, the more people will buy your products.

CHAPTER 13: SEO PHILOSOPHY

498. "There's a part of me that feels like enough is enough with the list of prohibited linking activities. I wish you'd just not count the links you don't think deserve credit." – Danny Sullivan

This was written in the comments section of a blog post by Matt Cutts (Head of Webspam at Google and responsible for Panda and Penguin) which said that guest blogging is over, and is a dodgy linkbuilding practice. With so many "prohibited forms of linkbuilding" out there, it's quite frustrating to see the list getting longer.

There shouldn't be a list, only common sense. If you think a certain blog is okay to get a backlink from, do it. If you think a link directory looks a little off-putting, don't do it.

499. "Those who have real empathy for web users and influencers AND have the SEO skills to infuse their work with great keyword targeting, search accessibility, etc., are going to have ongoing success." – Rand Fishkin

If I were to summarize SEO in one sentence, this quote from Rand sums it up beautifully. SEO may first appear to be a complex task that only tech geeks would understand, but when you break it down, it's quite doable.

500. You're Capable of Anything

Wahoo! This is the final tip, in the entire book.
And it required a lot of thought.

After all, I had to pick a tip which reflected the entire book whilst concluding it at the same time. And it's this:

You're capable of anything.

This tip sounds more like a piece of "real" philosophy rather than SEO philosophy.

But, it's true both in the real world and the SEO world.

If you want to start a successful website, SEO is the strategy that will get you there. Since the internet dominates our entire lives, SEO is actually a method to leading a successful life.

Put your mind to it, and you can do anything.

The Definitive Guide To Getting Published On Forbes, Life Hacker, The Huffington Post and 15 Other Famous Blogs (That Are Looking For Guest Writers Right Now)

The results of getting published on a major site like The Huffington Post or Forbes is unimaginable.
The Huffington Post gets about 250 million views every *month*. By writing even one article for them, your website and business will be put in front of a *massive* audience.

Your article wouldn't get tens, or hundreds or even, thousands of readers. Your article could, and probably would, get hundreds of thousands of readers.

Every author is allowed to place a link to their website, social media profile or product. Imagine how that would impact on your SEO! You'd get a VERY high value backlink to your site, and thousands of new customers in referral traffic.

Most writers that got published saw a life changing effect on their book/product sales, email subscribers and a lot of them even got famous.

Want to get published?

That's the problem.

Major websites like Forbes and Fast Company get THOUSANDS of pitches, EVERY DAY.

And the worst part?

Nobody reads them. So, if you're looking to get published, your pitch will end up in a slushy pile of lame pitches that no one will ever lay eyes on. However, I've been published on The Huffington Post and I've found out the step by step process to getting published.

And it's easier than you think. All you have to do is read this guide I've written.

What You'll Get

- The exact step by step process to getting published on websites with millions of monthly readers
- The contact details of the editors of these major sites that are looking for guest authors right now
- 3 email templates to pitch them the right way
- The step by step guide to writing a post that they'll love

How To Get The Guide

All you have to do is write a quick and honest review of this book on Amazon. Liked it? Loved it? Did it help your website? A quick few sentences is all that's needed. Send the link/screenshot of your review to me at seotips@yahoo.ie and you'll get the guide!

Want Me To Write On Your Blog?

If you find that content marketing takes too much time out of your day or you simply need some blog posts to get even more traffic to your site, I'll write them for you.

As you can see from all those content marketing tips, I know a LOT on content marketing. I've written posts that got 12,000 pins on Pinterest and collectively, all my guest posts have generated over 260,000 views online. I'm also starting a content marketing company in the future, so I need to know if there's going to be a demand for it.

Most experienced content marketers charge hundreds for their guest posts or consultations. Who seriously wants to pay that amount of money? And if you want to go cheap, you can pay $10 for a blog post that is short, unappealing and probably the latest creation from a spinning machine.

Contact me at seotips@yahoo.ie and let me know what content you want. Basically, my blog posts combine powerful SEO with viral social media tactics to get you the traffic your website deserves.

They're cheap too. It's **$50** for an ultimate guide (a linkable asset) that'll earn you money and leads for years to come, at 2500 words. Infused with all the latest 2015 SEO strategies and viral social media tactics.

Thank You For Reading!

Dear Reader,

I hope you have found this book to be useful.

SEO will change your website around forever. The power of search is limitless and it's accelerating exponentially each year.

I really hope that *500 SEO Tips* has helped you to achieve your goals and to get your website "out there". I've often found that simple tips and consolidated advice works best, so that's why this book came to be. It's about having dedicated readers like you which makes writing so enjoyable.

I need to ask you a favor. If you're so inclined, I'd be honored if you can write a review of this book.

Reviews are what can make or break a book these days, and you have the power to do that. I'm hoping to write more books which will give even more insanely actionable advice for getting more traffic, eg: something in the social media or conversion sphere. Your reviews will help me to write more books which will change digital marketing forever. Plus, you'll get the free guide to getting published on Forbes, and other major sites too.

If you have any questions or need some free SEO

advice, I'd be more than willing to help out. Just send me the link to your website and I'll give you some quick tips to improve your SEO.

Thank you so much for reading *500 SEO Tips* and for spending time with me. I'm certain that I'll see you and your website around. Who knows, we may cross paths again someday!
With gratitude,

Silvia O'Dwyer

**For feedback, questions, advice, sending reviews and requesting of content for your blog, contact Silvia below.
Email:** seotips@yahoo.ie

Printed in Great Britain
by Amazon.co.uk, Ltd.,
Marston Gate.